Barcelona

Architecture guide

Barcelona
Architecture guide

H KLICZKOWSKI

Idea and concept: **Paco Asensio and Hugo Kliczkowski**

Editor and texts: **Llorenç Bonet**

Editorial coordination: **Haike Falkenberg**

Photographs: **Roger Casas**

Translation: **Matthew Clarke**

Art director: **Mireia Casanovas Soley**

Graphic design: **Emma Termes Parera**

Layout: **Gisela Legares Gili, Soti Mas-Bagà**

Copy-editing: **Raquel Vicente Durán**

Copyright for the international edition:
© H Kliczkowski-Onlybook, S.L.
La Fundición, 15. Polígono Industrial Santa Ana
28529 Rivas-Vaciamadrid. Madrid, Spain
Tel.: +34 91 666 50 01
Fax: +34 91 301 26 83
onlybook@onlybook.com
www.onlybook.com

Editorial project:
2003 © LOFT Publications
Via Laietana 32, 4° Of. 92
08003 Barcelona, Spain
Tel.: +34 932 688 088
Fax: +34 932 687 073
loft@loftpublications.com
www.loftpublications.com

ISBN: 84-96241-65-3
DL: B-07479-04
Printed by:
Anman Gràfiques del Vallès, Barcelona, Spain

2004

Summary

Summary

Summary

Introduction

Barcelona is a densely populated city situated on a small plain between the sea and the Collserola mountain range. An old town with the Rambla as its main axis. The outlying towns annexed by the city in the 19th century–Sant Martí, Gràcia, Sarrià, Sants–are now neighborhoods with a character of their own. The Eixample (enlargement) designed by Cerdà serves as a dynamic mesh that allows for many different uses. The housing developments that grew up as a periphery in the 1960s and 1970s have today been integrated into the city. The ring roads with their heavy traffic surrounded and defined the city in the 1990s. The city-territory that we can now see owes its existence to the co-operation of surrounding towns–Badalona and Hospitalet, but also Mataró, Terrassa and Vilafranca del Penedès. Barcelona is a territory, an artificial environment, an accumulation of history, a corner in the Mediterranean, which can only grow by means of a network that is articulated with the collaboration of other cities, from Lisbon to Rome, from Seville to Brussels.

Barcelona awakens a series of ideas in the mind of an architect, and these have been expressed in many different forms. The Barcelona School, as the prestigious Architecture Faculty is known, gave its name to a group of architects who trained and presented their findings there in the sixties and seventies (from Ignasi Solà-Morales to Rafael Moneo); the Group R fomented the dialogue between Spain and the rest of Europe in the fifties (Antoni Moragas, José Antonio Coderch and Francisco J. Barba Corsini); the Group of Catalan Architects and Technicians for the Progress of Contemporary Architecture (GATCPAC), pioneered the modern movement through Josep Lluís Sert, Sixt Illescas, Germán Rodríguez Arias, Josep Torres i Clavé; Modernism, spearheaded by Lluís Domènech i Montaner and Antoni Gaudí, is one of the city's main tourist attractions, while the Eixample devised by the engineer Ildefons Cerdà has impinged on many of the architectural projects drawn up over the last 150 years.

"Despite its Rambla planted with trees and its beautiful straight streets, Barcelona has a somewhat rigid and dense air, like all cities surrounded too tightly by a fortified wall."

Théophile Gautier, "Journey to Spain", 1848

Barcelona is a Mediterranean city in the south of Europe, with a lay of the land that makes it difficult to expand; a city that wants to be a capital but cannot be, that needs to continuously reinvent itself. The 1992 Olympic Games provided it with a bold excuse to find its place in the world: it became a tourist destination that has since grown in popularity year by year. Also, the celebration of Forum 2004 in the city increased both the number of visitors and the resulting revenue, as it was an event that attracted not only tourists but also companies and facilities for business people.

"It proved strange to see the sea in Barcelona. The city and the Mediterranean had always been separated by the railroad tracks and dirty freight wagons, and on the beaches, polluted by the waste from the Lebon gas factory, by hundreds of squalid shacks that made up the so-called Somorrostro, where some twenty thousand people were crammed together."

Andreu Martín, 'La mujer del valiente' en "Barcelona, un dia"
('The Wife of the Brave Man' in "Barcelona, a day"), 1998

The opening-up of squares and avenues in the historic city has been a subject of fierce controversy in recent years, as these transformations have brought with them the destruction of the medieval city lay-out and the displacement of much of the population due to the uncontrollable rise in property prices.

Barcelona: a spectacular city that operates with catchwords and slogans, that sometimes portrays itself more as a store window than as a reality. An architectural challenge, a social debate. A metropolis somewhat erratic in its movements, like all cities, like any other living organism.

"In the space of three decades we have passed from a tormented city that gave rise to desperation and resentment to another one that has largely recovered its urban quality. The image of the city has also changed. From the besieged capital of the late seventies to the fun city of post-modernity, to the metropolis that is seeking its place in the world."

Julià Guillamon, "La ciutat interrompuda"
("The Interrumpted City"), 2000

Sant Pau del Camp Convent

The first references to Sant Pau del Camp date back to the 10th century, but it is thought to be older–it has even been suggested that the convent was founded in the 5th century.

Its façade still retains some Visigoth elements, despite the fact that the main structure is largely the result of reconstruction undertaken between the 11th and 13th century, along with later additions, such as the 18th-century octagonal tower. The Romanic structure, in the layout of a Greek cross, with three apses and a dome on scallops, was partly inspired by the interest in archeology that swept Europe in the 19th century. A fire in 1835 led to calls for the convent's demolition, but the first wave of intellectuals concerned with their heritage opposed this move and successfully campaigned for it to be declared a national monument. From then on the original Romanic structure prevailed over all other considerations, and as a result a 17th-century chapel was removed in 1922 because it masked the main façade. Later on, all the outhouses backing on to the building were demolished to leave the monument unobstructed, and this is how it looks today.

Architect: Unknown

Location: Carrer Sant Pau, 101

Date: 11-14th century

See map 1

Chapel of Sant Llàtzer

This large chapel (25 ft x 66 feet) formed part of the leper colony that was built on the outskirts of the city in the 12th century by Bishop Torroja. The growth of the Raval neighborhood and its inclusion within a new stretch of the wall in the 14th century integrated this hospice for lepers into the city, although in 1906 the service was transferred to the neighborhood of Horta.

In 1821 the building was refurbished and the surrounding area was converted to its present-day configuration, with the atrium that once gave access to the chapel being eliminated to open up the Plaça del Pedró. The City Hall gave permission to build on Carrer Hospital, on account of the city's mushrooming population, and part of the Romanic construction was hidden in the process. In 1913 it ceased to be a place of worship and was allowed to deteriorate.

Its interior retains a false vault dating from the 18th century; the exterior, distinguished by its apse, is cramped by the surrounding buildings. The present appearance of the chapel reflects the city's sprawl and superimposition of functions and architectural styles.

Architect: Unknown

Location: Plaça del Pedró, 2 bis

Date: 1141-1171

See map 1

Church of Sant Maria del Pi

This church has a single nave covered by rib vaulting and small side chapels. Its dimensions—179 feet long by 53 feet wide by 90 feet high—illustrate the southern Gothic form of religious architecture, which does not strive for verticality or a monumental scale. The seven sections of rib vaulting are supported by sturdy side buttresses, the bases of which are used to mark out the side chapels.

The main façade is distinguished by its austerity, as its only openings are a large rose window and a door whose decoration backs against the wall without attempting to hide the stretch of wall that extends with barely an interruption. Two small moldings run along the whole façade: the lower one—where the decoration on the door ends—marks the line covering the side chapels, while the upper one—framed by the upper third of the rose window—traces the roofs of the central nave. This device emphasizes the horizontality and is the only decorative element in this building, whose personality is expressed via the architectural mass. Its interior is the prototype of Catalan Gothic architecture.

Architects: Francesc Basset (1443) and Guillem Abiell (1415)

Location: Plaça del Pi, s/n.

Date: 1322-1508

See map 1

Pedralbes Monastery

This historical-artistic complex has preserved the characteristics of an isolated monastery, even though it has lost some of its defining elements, such as the boundary wall that protected all the buildings.

The monastery's church is typical of southern Gothic buildings, with its sober lines, emphasis on horizontality at the expense of verticality and uninterrupted stretches of wall instead of openings. French Gothic design influenced the unitary spatial conception, as opposed to the separation of spaces by means of heights or interruptions to the main nave. This single-nave building adapts to the terrain, thereby introducing slight variations from the traditional structure of other churches. The main entrance is not placed at the end opposite the main altar but in one of the sides, alongside the large clock tower. This innovative configuration overlooks a square.

Other interesting features of the monastery are the chapter house and the cloister, 150 ft long and three stories high (the first two from the 14th century), but most striking of all is its strictly rational basis of the organization.

Architect: Unknown. Chapter house:
Antoni Nató and Guillem Abiell, 1419

Location: Carrer Baixada del Monestir, 9

Date: 1326

See map 3

Church of Santa Maria del Mar

This church was made possible by the contributions of the shipping merchants who were based in this wealthy neighborhood. Considering its dimensions, it was built over a brief period (55 years), and it became one of the most striking and outstanding symbols of the city's seafaring power.

The church has three naves with side chapels and four stretches of rib vaulting in the roof. The central nave is square, and the other two are half its size. The ambulatory of the apse follows the general scheme of the rest of the church, despite its oblique outlines. All the elements have simple proportions and are interrelated, endowing the interior with a refinement and harmony: for example, the height of the central nave is similar to the width of the church; the vaults of the central nave are twice the size of the side ones; and the line which marks the start of the vaults of these side naves is half the height of the central one, and it is marked by capitals and a simple molding. The small gap in the height between the central and side naves makes up a static, unitary space in the interior that complements the smooth octogonal pillars, the chapels and the minimal decorative motifs.

Architects: Berenguer de Montagut, Guillem Metge
and Ramon Despuig

Location: Plaça de Santa Maria, s/n.

Date: 1329-1384

See map 1

Church of Sant Just and Pastor

This church was built in the Roman quarter on top of an amphitheater, in one of the city's oldest areas. Its single nave with five sections of rib vaulting and a polygonal apse follows the typical forms of Catalan Gothic architecture, with a dominant horizontality, powerful, solid buttresses with no arches and heavy walls that emphasize the volumetric mass of the building.

The main facade was planned with an entrance surrounded by two windows looking on to the street, while higher up there is a repetition of the form of the main door, with a large window. The offset of this second floor is created by the gap between the roof of the chapels and the central nave, and this gap is echoed along the sides of the church. Despite various modifications and restorations, the facade has stayed close to the original design, and the church's austere, simple structure has influenced other Gothic buildings, such as Santa María del Mar or the side face of the Ajuntament of Barcelona.

Architect: Bernat Roca

Location: Plaça de Sant Just, 5-6

Date: 1342-1572

See map 1

This building rests on part of the old Roman wall; it is thought that the palace of the Visigoth kings occupied the same site. Ever since the building was first put up it has been subject to constant reconstruction and extensions, particularly in the 13th and 14th centuries, in the period of the greatest financial and political splendor of the crown of Catalonia and Aragon.

The main entrance is situated at one end of the Plaça del Rei and is linked to the royal chapel (consecrated to Saint Agatha) and the Saló del Tinell, one of the most emblematic Catalan Gothic buildings, which leads to the main rooms of the palace, all set around a central patio in keeping with Mediterranean tradition. The three main components of the complex—the chapel, the Saló del Tinell and the palace itself—form a U shape that bounds the square.

The Saló del Tinell (1359-1370) contains an expansive space without pillars, measuring 56 x 110 feet, constructed on the basis of six large diaphragm arches, interlinked by small piped vaults in the half supporting the greatest tension and buttresses visible from the square on the exterior. This space is one of the most important civil buildings with respect to the southern Gothic techniques, but also worthy of note are the chapel of Saint Agatha, the royal bedroom and the watchtower known as the Torre del Rei Martí, which monitored the ships entering the port.

Architects: Bertran de Riquer, Jaume del Rei, Pere Oliva and Guillem Carbonell

Location: Plaça del Rei, s/n.

Date: 11th-14th century

See map 1

Drassanes

This building is one of the few medieval dockyards still in existence, and it exemplifies the use of diaphragm arches as a technique for covering large spaces, which was extensively applied in the Levant region of Spain up to the 19th century. This technique was also adopted for the reconstruction undertaken in the 16th and 17th centuries. These continual interventions make it difficult to establish an exact chronology for the building, although the structure and its functioning follow the original layout.

The construction is organized in a series of different naves, with a structure comprising longitudinal beams (covered by double-sloping Arabic tiles) that interlink with the diaphragm arches running crosswise. The first building, which was put up between 1284 and 1348, must have had a rectangular floor space that opened on to the beach, with four towers in the corners. Of this primitive structure, two of these towers are still standing (one of them in superb condition), along with some sections of the building itself. Around 1378, King Pere "the Ceremonious" enlarged the complex with eight naves near the sea and others further inland, separated by a large courtyard; at the end of the century he added a further extension. At the beginning of the 15th century a new royal palace was put up next to the dockyards, as the land was largely free of construction. The remains of this unfinished project now provide the setting for the Museu Marítim, although the central section, which is twice as big as the others, dates from the 17th century.

Architects: Arnau Ferrer and Joan Jener

Location: Plaça del Portal de la Pau, 1

Date: 1378

See map 1

Basses de Sant Pere

Even though this building has been very badly preserved, it nevertheless displays all the elements characteristic of medieval Gothic houses, and the changes these have undergone over the centuries.

The social life revolved around a central patio. The ground floor contained the family's business premises, while the first floor was given over to domestic life. The two balconies are later enlargements of the initial openings, which were much smaller—the balcony as such did not appear until the 16th century. The building has retained an open gallery on one side and a small, robust tower with two lobed windows on the other. Although the doors have been modified, one of them still bears traces of an arch, which was possibly part of the main entrance.

This type of house is to be found in various parts of the old town. The most lavish are those on the Carrer Montcada, which was one of the richest in medieval Barcelona. The layout of the street and the presence of 14th-century houses similar to this one—such as the two houses with a structure based on the big palaces that now serve as the Museu Picasso—provide a contrast with the major developments that have sprung up around it. These have been heavily criticized, largely for the destruction of the city's architectural heritage, but also for the social problems derived from the expropriation and remodeling of whole neighborhoods.

Architect: Unknown

Location: Carrer Basses de Sant Pere, 4

Date: 14th century

See map 1

Casa de l'Ardiaca

This building, home to the Historical Archive of the City, has undergone numerous modifications. In the 1920s the houses that masked the Roman wall were demolished. Leaving visible the relatively good condition of the wall. The configuration of this complex is unusual and has come to form an essential part of the area around the Cathedral, with the section of aqueduct being the most emblematic feature.

The archdeacon Lluís Desplà was responsible for a major refurbishment of the cathedral's outhouses at the beginning of the 15th century. A desire to dignify the somewhat unassuming buildings led to the construction of an imitation of the period's aristocratic houses, with a central patio, although the narrow plot did not make it possible to follow the prevailing models and the patio was separated from the street only by a wall. However, the building did follow the standard layout: the noble dwelling on the upper floors, and the warehouses and workshops below. The hall of golden pineapples, famous for its meticulous craftsmanship, has been preserved from the old complex. The bridge that joined the building's tower to the Bishop's palace was knocked down in 1822, and the chapel that Desplà had built nearby was absorbed to form part of the Bishop's palace.

Architect: Unknown

Location: Carrer Santa Llúcia, 1

Date: 1479-1510

See map 1

Palau del Lloctinent

After the union of the Crown of Castille with Catalonia and Aragon, the former Palau Reial Major was divided into different institutions as Barcelona lost its status as the preferred court. The General Mayoralty and the Royal Audience maintained control over the offices of the Racional and the archives, which had been housed in the old palace but were now transferred to a new location. So a new building was put up in 1549 to provide both residential quarters for the palace and another area for administrative functions.

The rectangular building stands unassumingly between the cathedral and the old royal palace; it has a symmetrical façade and its decoration is confined to the doors and windows, in keeping with Catalan architectural tradition. The interior is organised around a spacious central patio with an imposing staircase. The interior decoration of the palace corresponds to the esthetics of the Italian Renaissance, with half-circumference arches on the first-floor gallery supported by Tuscan pillars and embellished with lavish craftwork. The façade, however, is characteristic of Gothic art, with the dominance of uninterrupted stretches of wall and the absence of orders. Although their styles may differ, they both date from the same period.

Architect: Antoni Carbonell

Location: Carrer Comtes, 2/Plaça del Rei, s/n.

Date: 1549-1557

See map 1

Palau de la Generalitat

This building reflects the constant addition of small extensions over the course of hundreds of years, which makes its layout very irregular but bears witness to a very rich architectural heritage.

The Generalitat was first housed in a small building in carrer Sant Honorat, of which the general structure and two of the rooms remain today. At the beginning of the 15th century work began on the refurbishment that marked the beginning of the palace that can be seen today. Particularly striking is the construction of the façade in carrer Bisbe, designed by Marc Safont, which is one of the city's most significant secular Gothic constructions and served as the palace's main façade for two centuries. The same master was responsible for the entrance courtyard, the staircase with a loggia and the chapel of Sant Jordi. In the 16th century new outbuildings were added to the palace, and two orchards were combined to create the patio with orange trees, which is the showpiece of this building phase.

The year 1595 saw the start of the construction of the building's southern side–now the main façade on the Plaça Sant Jaume–and the Sant Jaume hall, both very important and scarce examples of the Renaissance forms bestowed on the city by the architect Pere Blai.

Construction has continued on a regular basis until the present day, but the late medieval structure of the palace has always been respected.

Architects: Marc Safont and Pere Johan (1416-1418) and Pere Blay (1596-1617)

Location Plaça de Sant Jaume, 4

Date: 1416-1418 (façade and a Gothic section) and 1596-1617

See map 1

Church of Betlem

The Church of Betlem was one of a series of buildings owned by the Jesuits in this part of the Rambla. It is one of the few examples in Barcelona of Catholic architecture dating from after the Council of Trent, although the original Baroque interior decoration can no longer be seen, as the church was damaged by a fire in 1936.

This church follows the trend started by Il Gesù, built in Rome by Il Vignola from 1568 to 1573 and one of the most popular models after the Council of Trent, although the concept of the transept is dispensed with here and the decoration on the façade follows that of churches built after Il Gesù. There is a single nave, completed by a semicircular apse next to the altar, with seven sections of equal length and a smaller one adjacent to the main entrance, once occupied by a large organ. To the sides of this nave large chapels open up, interlinked by large doors that set up a second directional axis parallel to the central nave, as if there were lateral naves. It is worth noting the similarities between this approach and the examples of southern Gothic to be found in Barcelona.

Architect: Josep Juli

Location: La Rambla, 107/Carrer Carme, 2-4

Date: 1681-1732

See map 1

Church of Sant Felip Neri

The Church of Sant Felip Neri originally belonged to the Convent of the Clergues Seculars de l'Oratori, an order created in Barcelona in the mid-17th century in keeping with the precepts of the precepts of the Treaty of Trent. The present building was put up one hundred years later, and like most Post-Tridentine churches it follows the model of Il Gesù de Vignola, with a central nave with deep intercommunicating chapels, a short transept, a crucifer covered with a large vault and a semicircular apse. The façade has simple lines, with a closed wall that is only decorated around the door and two enormous pilasters that support the upper cornice and indicate the breadth of the central nave in the interior. The Church of the Ciutadella influenced the building's semicircular top, and the oculus between this and the façade functions as a transition between these two elements.

The square in front of the church retains the fountain that once provided the neighborhood's water supply, as well as serving for washing clothes. The two buildings that close the square at an angle in front of the church are both reconstructions from the mid-20th century.

Architects: Unknown (probably Pere Bertran and Salvador Ausich i Font)

Location: Plaça de Sant Felip Neri, s/n.

Date: 1748-1752

See map 1

Neighborhood of Barceloneta

The neighborhood of Barceloneta was built to rehouse the inhabitants of the Born. The first plan was drawn up in 1715 by Próspero de Verboom, and the homes were initially built of wood and brick.

The Engineer General Juan Martín Cermeño was responsible for a new project in 1753. This planned long, narrow plots that marked a directional axis leading toward the Ciutadella, with eleven streets running in this direction, occasionally crossed by others. It also foresaw facilities like a church and a market. The houses were to be single-story buildings with a tiled roof, with a total floor area of 1,075 square ft; they all had the same dimensions, designed according to the plans of the Engineer General. The demographic pressure was continually increasing—with a total of 1,300 inhabitants—and this created a social problem for the city. In 1839 the Governor agreed to the addition of another story and presented a model that was very similar to the original plan. By 1868 the regulations permitted a third story and an attic. The buildings have continued to increase in height over the years, and as a result it is now difficult to find sunny streets in this closely packed neighborhood.

Architect: Juan Martín Cermeño

Location: Neighborhood of Barceloneta

Date: 1753

See map 1

Casa dels Velers

This house is the headquarters of the trade guild responsible for veils, silks and other sophisticated textiles. The building forms a rectangular block, with the main entrance on Carrer Sant Pere més Alt, where most of the shops selling these types of textiles are concentrated. After the opening of Via Laietana in 1931, the lateral face became more prominent than the smaller main façade, as the former overlooked the broad new street, which grew to be the financial heart of the city. The preservation of the building can be credited to Jeroni Martorell, the head of the department that catalogued and conserved the city's monuments, who fought to avoid the building's demolition as a result of the configuration of the new street. Thanks to his efforts, it was declared a national monument in 1916.

Both façades are decorated with sgraffito, and they are considered the best example of this technique in Barcelona, both for their quality and for the refinement of their iconography, replete with classical allusions. The corner balcony, embellished with the image of the guild's patron saint, unifies the stretches of wall on the two façades.

Architect: Joan Garrido i Bertrán

Location: Via Laietana, 50

Date: 1758-1763

See map 1

Llotja de Barcelona

This was built in 1383 in order to create a space worthy of the trading operations that took place in the city. The market originally included not only the trading hall but also a patio with orange trees, a chapel and outbuildings that were added as required; only the trading hall has been preserved. The medieval market must have resembled the one in Valencia, although that was made of stone with a vault and the one in Barcelona was built with diaphragm arches and a flat wooden roof, like the Saló del Tinell.

The current building derives from a far-reaching city-planning scheme that embraced not only a bigger market—as the old one was in a poor condition—but a reordering of the link between the port and the city. The Neoclassical complex absorbed the Gothic structure by integrating it as one of the outhouses. This mixture is barely perceptible in the absolutely regular façade, as only one small detail betrays the asymmetry that lies within: the central part of the longitudinal façade is set off by a tympanum and a wide balcony, but there is no entrance on the lower floor.

Architects: Pere Albei (1381) and Joan Soler i Faneca (1764)

Location: Pla de Palau/Passeig d'Isabel II, s/n.

Date: 1381 and 1764-1802

See map 1

Palau de la Virreina

Manuel Amat, the viceroy in Peru, sent the plans for this house from Lima with very precise and detailed technical instructions. However, these designs had to be adjusted to the somewhat irregular dimensions of the plot, as the original project envisaged a square layout. The building is set back from the other buildings, as the alignment of the street was not decided until 1776–by which time the façade had already been built. The walls of the Rambla were not demolished until the mid-18th-century, which is why it has no great noble or middle-class palaces, despite the fact that it is the widest street in Barcelona.

The palace is laid out around a long interior corridor–with access from both the Rambla itself and a backstreet–which leads to an inner patio that receives sunlight, allowing it to pour into all the rooms. The decoration of the façade and the wrought-iron elements follow French models, although these are merged with traditional local features, such as the large pottery urns. The entire building is distinguished by its stone carvings, most especially on the interior double staircase, where the Tuscan capitals are adapted to the oblique forms of this vertical walkway.

Architects: Manuel Amat, Josep Ausich and Carles Grau

Location: La Rambla, 99

Date: 1772-1778

See map 1

Parc del Laberint d'Horta

Joan Antoni Desvalls i d'Ardena was an example of a well-educated, enlightened humanist. He dreamed up the idea for the gardens in his family's country house (one of the few Romantic gardens in Barcelona). The grounds also include the Torre Sobirana, a farmhouse that was known to exist in the 7th century but was radically overhauled in the mid-19th-century in an Arabian style. This refurbishment, one of the first Neo-Arab projects in the city, followed the dictates of European fashion at the time, and this trend also went on to interest the Modernist architects.

The garden is popularly known as the Maze of Horta, but in fact only one part of the extensive series of terraced gardens contains a maze. In all, this Romantic garden boasts a false cemetery, a navigable pond and canal and an expansive garden lined with paths designed to emphasize the perspectives and set up the concept of a route. According to Professor Federico Revilla, the project was conceived as a playful, initiating path through different kinds of love, as represented by the allegorical figures (Eros, Venus, Echo and Narcissus) set at strategic points in the garden.

Architects: Domenico Bagutti and Andreu Valls

Location: Passeig de la Vall d'Hebron, s/n.

Date: 1793-1804

See map 3

Palau Alós

This building from the early 19th century tried to adapt a very austere neoclassical approach to the typical layout of a Barcelona mansion house, with a central patio connecting the different parts of the interior. A comparison with the mansion in Carrer Canuda, built in 1796 and now the home of Barcelona's Ateneu, shows both the persistence of the patio and, above all, a certain evolution of the classical idiom, as in the earlier building the elements that articulate the wall form part of the classical repertoire –pediments in the windows and cornices on each floor–while in Carrer Sant Pere més Alt these elements have disappeared almost completely. So, the Palau Alós only marks the horizontal plane with a large balcony on the first floor, heavy bonding on the ground floor and a cornice on the top, while its vertical lines are marked by a slight modulation in the wall that does not draw on the classical order.

To understand this sobriety, it is perhaps important to bear in mind the widespread dissemination of the rigorist ideas of Francesco Milizia expressed in "Principi di Architettura Civile" (1785) and "Dizionario delle Belle Arti del Disegno" (1797), which may have exerted an influence on 19th-century architecture in Barcelona.

Architect: Unknown

Location: Carrer Sant Pere més Alt, 27

Date: 1807-1818

See map 1

Ajuntament de Barcelona

The original Ajuntament or Casa de la Ciutat was a body that had greater powers than a modern City Hall; it was housed in a building which, like that of the Generalitat, has been marked by different phases of construction. The main door of the Gothic building (1399-1402) can still be seen today. The inner patio—now incomplete as a result of later construction—follows the scheme of a local aristocratic house and leads on to the Saló del Consell de Cent (1373), an expansive space with no supports and two large diaphragm arches. The building also boasted an orchard with orange trees and the Saló del Trentenari, but these were both destroyed as part of the extensive refurbishment undertaken in the 19th century, which involved the construction of new rooms and the enlargement of the Saló de Cent. These alterations began after the fire in the chapel of Sant Jaume in 1822; its subsequent demolition made it possible to open up a large square between the Ajuntament and the Generalitat. This led to a new façade (1830-1847) with Neoclassical lines; this is somewhat heavy and static, despite the device of a protruding block with four freestanding Ionic pillars. This new façade led to the destruction of the previous façade and various Gothic rooms, as well as the reduction in the size of the patio.

Architects: Arnau Bargués (Gothic façade), Pere Llobet
(Saló del Consell de Cent) and Josep Mas i Vila
(Neoclassical façade)

Location: Plaça de Sant Jaume, s/n.

Date: 1373-1402 and 1831-1855

See map 1

Casas d'en Xifré

This block provided a coherent concept for building houses in front of the Llotja de Barcelona, in one of the first enlargements drawn up for the city. As land for construction was in short supply, the demolition of the walls by the sea and the development of this area attracted merchants and other people with means, and the resulting area proved more open than the rest of the medieval city, with wider streets and bigger patios.

This residential complex is divided into five distinct sections, with large porticos that give on to the two-story commercial premises. The longitudinal expanse of the façade is decorated with Ionic pilasters, six of which form a central block that serves as a vertical axis while two at each end help to give the sides of the building a sharply defined edge. These side pilasters are each topped by a small cupola, while a tiered tympanum with a group of sculptures—a Vanitas—rounds off the central block.

The complex was built at a time when the Isabelline style was enjoying its greatest glory.

Architects: Josep Boixareu and Francesc Vila

Location: Passeig d'Isabel II, 14

Date: 1836-1840

See map 1

Gran Teatre del Liceu

The Liceu is an opera house set in the heart of the city. For many years it symbolized the prestige of Barcelona's bourgeoisie, as it was one of the biggest theaters in Europe when it was built and, furthermore, it was financed entirely by private capital—in other words, without any help from the State, which explains the absence of a royal box, even though Spain was a monarchy at that time.

The Liceu was built on an irregular plot that was formerly the sight of a Trinitarian convent; the main façade is on the Rambla. The model that was followed for the stage and concert hall was the Scala in Milan, but the Barcelona version is bigger.

The general plan drawn up by Miquel Garriga i Roca was been maintained, despite the many interventions and refurbishments that it has undergone as a result of two devastating fires (1861 and 1994), which made it necessary to meticulously reconstruct the original project. The theater was enlarged after the last fire, with the aid of generous investment from the Catalan administration, and its seats were no longer reserved for particular fee-paying patrons but became open to all.

Architects: Miquel Garriga i Roca and Josep Oriol i Mestres

Location: La Rambla, 61-65

Date: 1845-1947

See map 1

Plaça Reial

The opening-up of the Plaça Reial and Carrer Ferran at the beginning of the 19th century were development schemes of capital importance to the city, which still had a medieval layout lacking in large squares and straight streets. As soon as they were built, this square and street became favorite spots for the bourgeoisie and members of the new liberal professions that sprung up after the emergence of the universities and centers of higher education.

The square was built on the site of a former Capuchin convent, which had been destroyed after the selling-off of church property by Mendizábal in 1835. The project fitted in with the urban fabric and skilfully connected pre-existing streets with the new square, although it was not possible to achieve a perfect symmetry and the square is slightly trapezoidal in form. The links with the surrounding streets were brilliantly realized by means of porticos, especially in the cases of the Passatge Madoz, which takes the form of a patio, and the Passatge Bacardí (1856), which is protected by glass roofs.

Architect: Francesc Daniel Molina i Casamajó

Location: Plaça Reial

Date: 1848

See map 1

Boqueria Market

In 1836 a plan was drawn up to build the Plaça de Sant Josep on the site of an old convent for barefoot Carmelite nuns. Construction work began in 1840 but was never completed, and the market was eventually built on the site. The initial plan foresaw a square with porticos, with the novelty that these porticos were crowned by private gardens extending from the first stories of the surrounding apartments. Today part of this unfinished square remains, albeit half-hidden by the market, and the most recent refurbishment sought to recover the porticos, which had been occupied by stores.

The market is an iron structure with longitudinal naves that is as simple as it is effective. Its outstanding feature is the entrance from the Rambla, with a large iron arch inlaid with stained glass. Also striking are some of the market stalls dating from Barcelona's golden age of Modernism, which have been preserved in all their glory until the present day. The last refurbishment, in 2003, not only restored the old porticos but also gave rise to a small office building to the rear, where provision was also made for the disposal of garbage.

Architect: Josep Mas i Vila

Location: La Rambla, 105

Date: 1860

See map 1

Placeta Milans

This small square was one of the urban developments undertaken in the 19th century. Although as a whole it does display a certain unity, the contours, traced with simple lines, were not the result of a continuous period of construction, as the required permission to enlarge the site was refused by the military authorities, who were the final arbiters in such matters.

The Palau neighborhood owes its name to the monarchs' smaller palace, which was knocked down in the middle of the 19th century. The land was used to build spacious houses and it grew into a wealthy neighborhood. The planning of the Placeta Milans resulted from the desire to give a distinctive touch to the street that linked the Palau neighborhood with Carrer Avinyó, a street with middle-class residences typical of Barcelona. The octagonal layout of the square was intended to create a space that was larger than an ordinary street and thereby give more room to the façades of the houses, so that they could receive more sunlight and ventilation. Moreover, it provided a simple way of organizing the street along geometrical lines, in an area where it was impossible to put a thoroughfare running along straight lines.

Architect: Francesc Daniel Molina

Location: Carrer Milans

Date: 1849-1870

See map 1

Universitat de Barcelona

Barcelona's tradition of higher education, dating back to the Middle Ages, was interrupted in 1717 when Philip V transferred the university to Cervera after the War of Succession. Not until 1846 was the possibility of restoring Barcelona its university status considered again, after an initiative from the Court. From the outset Elies Rogent i Amat campaigned to get the university back and in the 1850s he searched for the ideal plot, both within and outside the city walls. He finally opted for land close to the historic city but within the grid of the Eixample drawn up by Cerdà.

Rogent i Amat, who went on to be the first head of Barcelona's University of Architecture, used the Neo-Gothic idiom to design this building spread over two blocks in the Eixample. The main façade, 425 feet long, marks out the three units that make up the building and the two cloistered patios that separate them. A further patio to the rear provides an area for relaxation and leisure activities, whereas the two inner patios serve to distribute the space.

The most imposing feature of the building is the paranymph and the impressive steps and gallery leading to it. Its decoration with medieval and Islamic-based elements follows the ideas of Violet-le-Duc in its investigation of all types of architecture—not just the Classical model—and the search for a solid technical base for buildings.

Architect: Elies Rogent

Location: Gran Via de les Corts Catalanes, 5

Date: 1862-1873

See map 1

Passatge Permanyer

The Passatge Permanyer is an example of the difficult and varied implementation of the city planning ideas formulated by Idefons Cerdà for the Eixample of Barcelona. Although in the early stages he foresaw construction on only a third of each block, he eventually opted for a more densely populated model of city, in keeping with the financial reality of the times. This passage is one of the few that were designed on a unified basis and the only one that has conserved its appearance, although most of the houses are now used as offices. The architect lined this passageway with terraced one-story houses fronted by a small garden, as the regulations did not permit the buildings to be any higher. This design along English lines was complemented by Arab-style decorative features, typical of the period.

The passage in the middle of a block was the only model that evaded the concept of a closed block with buildings on all four sides. The City Hall is currently trying to recover the patios inside the blocks as public spaces, with initiatives like the Gardens of the Torre de les Aïgues on Carrer Llúria, just opposite this passage.

Architect: Jeroni Granell i Barrera

Location: Passatge Permanyer

Date: 1864

See map 2

Born Market

The former general market for fish and fresh produce is one of the most emblematic examples of construction with iron in the 19th century. The iron pillars of the structure support a metal framework covered with terracotta tiles—both cheap and easily mass-produced materials—to create a building that occupies almost all the rectangular plot. The roofs reflect the hierarchical organization of the space, with a dome and a short transversal nave that interrupt the path of the longitudinal nave—the result of a hybrid between a centralized layout and a more directional scheme. All the outer part of the building is bounded by a nave, and as this is lower than the rest it emphasizes the importance of the dome and the hierarchical organization of the different heights.

The layout of the market and its surroundings was the responsibility of Josep Fontserè, who managed to harmoniously connect the medieval city with this new area: the market, the Estació de França and the nearby port.

Architect: Josep Fontserè

Location: Plaça Comercial, 12

Date: 1883-1884

See map 1

Museu d'Història

This former trading depot was put up in the mid-19th century in one of the city's most economically dynamic districts.

The architect Elias Rogent fulfilled his commission along functional lines. He used brick to build a large rectangular building with three naves and a slightly smaller building facing the sea, designed for offices. The ground floor of this building is opened up by big arcades, an area with porticos and an interior passageway that crosses the entire building before emerging in the façade overlooking the city. This passageway not only neatly linked the quay to the city but also crossed the warehouse to provide an efficient means of unloading, storing and checking merchandise before it was distributed.

The structure comprises brick load-bearing walls with vaults on all the floors, except for the roof, where brick arches support a double-slope roof made of wood and tiles.

Architect: Elies Rogent

Location: Plaça de Pau Vila, 1

Date: 1874-1879

See map 1

Casas Fontserè

The plan to transform the military citadel into a park foresaw the use of part of the land to build houses, as both a means to pay for the new park and barracks and as compensation for the former owners of houses destroyed by the war in 1714.

The result was five blocks of varying dimensions with a uniform façade overlooking the Parc de la Ciutadella (in what is now the Passeig Picasso), with a large portico as an element of continuity between the blocks. Apart from their immaculately structured façade, these five blocks organize the transition between the old town and the rest of the city by means of a major vertical axis: Carrer Comerç, which directly links the Passeig de Lluís Companys with the medieval city and the Estació de França. Josep Fontserè also designed the blocks to fit into the layout of the old city's road network; Carrer Princesa was extended and a large, open-plan market was created at the end of the Passeig del Born. This area became the financial powerhouse of the neighborhood for over a century.

Architect: Josep Fontserè

Location: Carrer Comerç/Passeig Picasso

Date: 1874

See map 1

The original plan was for an unassuming grotto designed to hide the water tank that supplied the various fountains in the park, but the bourgeois bigwigs somehow managed to turn this modest project into an ambitious scheme that proclaimed the glory of the city. To do this, the design imitated that of the fountain in the Longchamp Palace in Marseilles, but on a bigger scale: a spectacular staircase surrounds the water, which is divided into two pools on different levels and culminates in a triumphal arch that that frames the main sculptural group and concentrates most of the allegorical sculptures, such as the crown and Aurora's chariot (a Republican symbol).

The upper part of the construction contains a freestanding block–reached by a bridge at the top of the staircase–that contains one of the park's main attractions: a grotto that picturesquely recreates the interior of a cave, complete with large stalactites. The young Antoni Gaudí worked as an apprentice in Fontserè's workshop during the construction of the waterfall and he absorbed the concept of the relationship between architecture and Nature as an inspiration for buildings.

Architect: Josep Fontserè

Location: Parc de la Ciutadella:
Passeig de Pujades

Date: 1875-1881

See map 1

Casa Vicens

In 1883 the young Gaudí took on one of his first commissions as an architect. This house still displays the straight lines that he would subsequently abandon in favor of curves and seemingly impossible forms, but the seeds of his later work are present in this distinctive, ostentatious building.

This house in the Gràcia neighborhood is imposing in its mixture of Spanish architectural forms, inspired by the medieval period but with striking Arab touches more proper to Mudejar art than the architecture prevalent at the time, which followed the trends of the French school. Despite the fact that the house had to be built on a plot of limited dimensions framed by traditional buildings, Gaudí's creation manages to be both distinctive and perfectly adapted to its surroundings. He conceived it as a subtle combination of geometrical volumes, skillfully achieved by the use of horizontal strips on the lower part of the building and vertical lines—emphasized by the ornamental varnished tiles—on the upper part. Gaudí chose simple materials for the exterior walls, such as natural, ocher-colored stone combined with brick.

Architect: Antoni Gaudí

Location: Carrer Carolines, 24-26

Date: 1883-1888

See map 2

Fundació Antoni Tàpies

This building, formerly occupied by the Montaner i Simon publishing house and print shop, was one of the first to make a clean break with historicist idioms. It used new construction materials in a rational manner, and it can therefore be considered one of the first modern buildings in Barcelona. It comprised a small office section, set in parallel with the façade, and a large workshop to the rear. The façade and the offices act as a screen between the street and the workshop, thereby disguising the industrial nature of the building. The structure of the workshop is very simple and functional, with iron pillars supporting two stories that are visually intercommunicated by a large gap in the flooring on the second story—making it possible for sunlight to penetrate the lower floor via the large skylights in the roof. The office section is also propped up by iron pillars, although the main focus of attention is the façade, with its exposed brickwork set off by large fixed windows.

The refurbishment undertaken by Roser Amadó and Lluís Domènech i Girbau in 1987 transformed the space but retained its most characteristic elements, as well as installing a large sculpture by Antoni Tàpies, "The Chair and the Cloud", on the roof of the Foundation.

Architect: Lluís Domènech i Montaner

Location: Carrer Aragó, 255

Date: 1881-1886

See map 2

Temple of the Sagrada Família

In 1887 the congregation of the devotees of Saint Joseph launched a project for the construction of a large temple financed by means of donations. The architect Francisco de Paula del Villar designed a Neo-Gothic church: three naves with a crypt set out in line with the plot's octagonal axes. In 1883, the architect relinquished his control of the construction works after disagreements with the board because his plans overran the proposed budget. Joan Martorell, the chairman of the board, recommended the young Gaudí, who took on the project when he was still only thirty-one.

In 1884 he drew up the elevation and cross-section of the altar of the Chapel of Saint Joseph, which was opened the following year. Gaudí dreamed up a church with numerous technical innovations, with the Latin-cross layout superimposed onto the original crypt. Above this, the main altar is surrounded by seven chapels consecrated to the trials and sins of Saint Joseph. The doors of the transept are devoted to Christ's Passion and Birth, while the main façade celebrates his Glory. Gaudí designed four towers above each façade—12 in all—to represent the apostles, with another one in the middle symbolizing Jesus, another four around this for the Evangelists and a further one dedicated to the Virgin.

Gaudí died on June 10, 1926, leaving the building unfinished; it is scheduled for completion in 2007.

Architect: Antoni Gaudí

Location: Plaça de la Sagrada Família, s/n.

Date: 1883-1926

See map 2

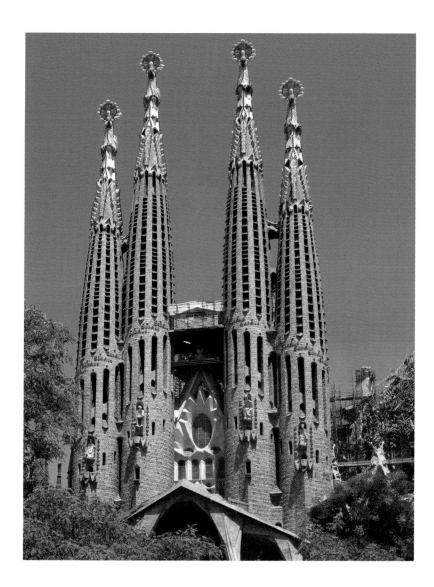

Casa Bruno Quadros

Josep Vilaseca i Casanovas regularly collaborated with Domènech i Montaner and shared his desire to revitalise architecture, as they both felt that it was failing to take advantage of the progress then being made in engineering and the applied arts.

Vila was responsible for refurbishing the 18th-century house: he designed a new façade and altered part of the interior. With this project he used an imaginative approach imbued with Oriental elements to try to break away from the dichotomy between the Neo-Gothic esthetic and eclecticism. The façade draws on the eclectic repertoire to solve the decoration of the windows, while the gallery on the top floor boasts thick pilasters that recall the pseudo-Egyptian motifs that swept Europe in the 19th century. This mixture sets off even more strongly the building's most distinctive decorative element: the parasols made from multi-colored ceramics, which are the origin of the building's popular name of the Casa de los Paraguas (house of umbrellas). Apart from referring directly to Bruno Quadros' umbrella store on the ground floor, this Oriental element, along with the large dragon set on the corner, makes this façade highly original.

Architect: Josep Vilaseca i Casanovas

Location: La Rambla, 82

Date: 1891-1896

See map 1

Umbracle

The Umbracle forms part of the cultural complex that was put up for the Universal Exhibition of 1888 and perfectly illustrates the 19th-century interest in classifying and giving scientific names to all living beings that was derived from the ideas of Encyclopedism. It is no accident that the Museu de Geologia stands alongside the Umbracle, which houses a collection of plants, and that close to these buildings there is a small zoo.

The building is made up of five naves with a roof straddled by semicircular metal hoops and wooden sheets, which are separated from each other to filter the rainwater and allow diffuse sunlight to enter. The iron supports are proof of the elegance and mastery of this construction system in the hands of Fontserè, who was one of the most interesting architects of this period, despite the fact that he had no academic training and was only a master builder. The simple but effective structure contrasts with the façade, built with elaborate brickwork, which was very fashionable in Barcelona at the time and gave a touch of class to a municipal building. This material went on to be very popular with Catalan Modernism.

Architect: Josep Fontserè

Location: Parc de la Ciutadella

Date: 1883-1884

See map 1

Palau Güell

The Palau Güell, which has been classified as a world heritage site by UNESCO, is the building that made Gaudí's name. He designed this residence on an unlimited budget, without skimping on materials: he used the best stone, the best wrought iron and the best woodwork, making it the most expensive house of the period.

The position of this urban mansion, in a narrow street in Barcelona's historic quarter, makes it difficult to view the building as a whole from the outside. Güell decided to make his home here for two reasons: to avoid giving up this family property and to improve the area's bad reputation. The sober stone façade belies the majestic interior, where Gaudí gave rein to an unaccustomed sumptuousness. The façade went through a total of over 25 designs before the definitive choice, which was configured along bold historicist lines, with some subtle classical touches. Two large doors in the form of a parabolic arch make up the entrance to the house, which is spread over a basement, four floors and a roof terrace. The basement is reached via two ramps, one for servants and the other for horses.

Architect: Antoni Gaudí

Location: Carrer Nou de la Rambla, 3-5

Date: 1886-1888

See map 1

Museu de Zoologia

This building was designed to be the café-restaurant of the Universal Exhibition but it was not finished in time. Even so, it is one of the most surprising and innovative buildings arising from the exhibition project, along with the same architect's central hotel (now unfortunately destroyed), a high-quality building that was put up with prefabricated iron structures in a mere 53 days.

What is surprising is the structure: the ground floor, which contains the large nave, is realized by means of two large metal arches, which form the skeleton, while the brick walls and arches round off the structure. This simple design (which is repeated on the first floor) creates expansive spaces that do not require intermediate supports, thereby demonstrating the architect's great technical skill. However, it is not clear whether this approach was inspired by the diaphragm arches of southern Gothic architecture or the contemporary engineering works made with iron, such as the bridges designed by Eiffel. The central gallery is flanked by two completely functional service wings that blend in harmoniously with the rest of the building.

Architect: Lluís Domènech i Montaner

Location: Passeig Pujades, s/n.

Date: 1887-188

See map 1

Palace of Justice

This sumptuous public building was drawn up with the intention of redefining the lower part of the Passeig de Sant Joan, which, around the time of the Universal Exhibition of 1888, seemed likely to become the city's second most important bourgeois boulevard, after the Passeig de Gràcia. Although these aspirations did not come to fruition, this project was completed, and it remains one of the few public buildings that does not make use of any pre-existing construction. It is designed in accordance with the ideas of the École de Beaux Arts in Paris, which were widely imitated throughout Europe in the 19th century. The concept of walls as a means for applied arts shows the influence of French and European Art Nouveau, although the overall idiom is eclectic.

The layout of the building follows the French style, with a central section acting as an axis of symmetry between the four inner patios and, around them, the galleries containing offices. The architects designed an extremely eye-catching axis starting from the main entrance, with a large staircase that leads up to the functions suite on the second floor, although the two smaller side staircases are used more often.

Architects: Josep Domènech i Estapà and Enric Sagnier i Villavecchia

Location: Passeig de Lluís Companys, 14

Date: 1887-1908

See map 1

Finca Güell

Eusebi Güell, Gaudí's principal patron, entrusted the architect with construction work on an estate between the neighborhoods of Les Corts and Sarrià. He was required to not only refurbish some preexisting buildings but also to create some other modules and additional elements and design various decorative complements.

The enormous grounds boast two entrance gates–one for pedestrians, the other for carriages. They are flanked by two pavilions: the gatekeeper's quarters and the stables, which are linked to another area that was used a riding-school. The gatekeeper's lodge was designed as a pavilion divided into three sections: the main one has an octagonal layout, while the other two are rectangular and back on to it. The stables comprise a single rectangular unit with parabolic arches and partitioned vaults. The trapezoidal openings allow in generous amounts of sunlight, which is intensified by the white of the walls. The lodge and the stables frame the large wrought-iron gate, inlaid with a representation of a dragon that was created in 1885 by the Vallet i Piquer workshop after a design by Gaudí.

Architect: Antoni Gaudí

Location: Avinguda Pedralbes/
Avinguda Joan XXIII

Date: 1884-1887

See map 3

Theresian School

The design for this college in Barcelona's Sant Gervasi was inevitably constrained by certain determining factors, such as the fact that the building was dedicated to Saint Teresa and that its community of Carmelite nuns had taken a vow of poverty.

Gaudí took on the project in March 1889, after some earlier construction for a planned group of three buildings had already been undertaken; this meant that he had to confront a ground floor and first st ory that had already been built. Gaudí adapted not only to the budget—more modest than he was accustomed to—and the guidelines established by his predecessor—some sections could not be modified—but also to the austerity, asceticism and sobriety required by the religious order. Without relinquishing his particular striking and imaginative style, Gaudí carried out an exercise of personal restraint and drew up a building of bold but controlled lines where moderation (unheard of in his previous work) is the main characteristic—at least in the forms, because a closer look reveals that the college is rich in symbolic elements.

The heavy supporting walls put up on the ground floor by means of parabolic arches were replaced by long symmetrical corridors on the upper levels, thus endowing the composition with great dynamism.

Architect: Antoni Gaudí

Location: Carrer Ganduxer, 85

Date: 1888-1889

See map 3

Casa Thomas

Domènech i Montaner drew up a two-story building crowned with two asymmetrical towers for the Thomas family, with a residence on the first floor and a print shop below it. The original design is reminiscent of the workshops of the old Montaner i Simon publishing house (now the Fundació Antoni Tàpies).

The façade was created with a large arch on the ground floor; this is flanked by two symmetrical doors, one for the print shop and one for the home. The arch was closed off with large panes of glass, allowing light to enter both the first floor and the basement; this set a precedent for the use of glass to cover large stretches of wall for functional purposes.

In 1912 Francesc Guàrdia i Vidal added three further stories. He moved the two towers to the new roof and largely retained the structure and certain elements of the second floor, by dismantling it and transferring it to the top.

In 1979 the Per studio refurbished the ground floor and basement to make way for the bd design store.

Architect: Lluís Domènech i Montaner

Location: Carrer Mallorca, 291

Date: 1895-1898

See map 2

Hidroeléctrica de Catalunya

In accordance with the usual scheme in Barcelona, the headquarters of the Hidroeléctrica de Catalunya united both offices and workshops in a single building, with the former in the front and the latter to the rear. The result illustrates the quality of the architects who were working in the city at the end of the 19th century. The approach recalls that of the headquarters of the old Montaner i Simon publishing house (now the Fundació Antoni Tàpies) in its use of brick and iron and in the placement of large windows in the first two floors. Falqués' building also introduces a new construction device: it uses the small iron girders in the fluting of the façade as reinforcing braces and not as direct supports for the structure.

The use of the attributes of brick to bring dynamism to the plane of a façade forms part of Barcelona's modern tradition, as illustrated by the nearby Arc de Triomf (Josep Vilaseca, 1888). However, this practice is exploited to excess in the Hidroeléctrica building and the resulting façade is heavy and overloaded. The project was unfinished; it was to have been crowned with bronze sculptures and two large pyramids—perhaps in allusion to the elements featured in the designs for industrial buildings by Ledoux.

Architect: Pere Falqués i Urpí

Location: Carrer Roger de Flor, 52

Date: 1896-1897

See map 1

La Rotonda

This building was put up in the middle of an area where many residences were being built, but it was the only one that tried to fit in with the city's layout by occupying the entire plot. Conscious of its emblematic layout at the bottom of Avinguda Tibidabo and the top of Carrer Balmes, Adolf Ruiz i Casamitjana drew up a circular tower for the corner to create a symbolic element in a neighborhood without any obvious reference points. The impact of the decorative dome on the top of the tower is enhanced by the profuse decoration of tiles and sculpted elements. The rest of the building displays similar ornamental flourishes, but the basic configuration of the building lacks the imagination expected of a Modernista building. The large terraces to the back of the building once enjoyed views of natural landscape, but the intense development has obscured most of these.

The imposing tower is not only a defining element of the Plaça Kennedy, it also marks the beginning of the route of the Tramvia Blau that provided the transport system for this residential area.

Architect: Adolf Ruiz i Casamitjana

Location: Passeig de Sant Gervasi, 51

Date: 1906-1908

See map 3

Casa Calvet

The Casa Calvet is tucked between two adjoining buildings on a street in the Eixample, in an area where the planning and use of the land marked out a rigidly standardized format for the buildings.

The owner kept for himself the first-floor apartment and a warehouse and office on the ground floor (currently occupied by a restaurant, which has preserved some of the original decorative motifs). The rest of the building was given over to rented apartments, all of which were designed on an individual basis. The exuberance of the entrance hall contrasts with the austerity of the main façade; this is formally more restrained than the rear and is defined on a single plane, with the masonry and carved stone giving it a rough texture that sets off the lobed wrought-iron balconies and various sculptural elements.

Antoni Gaudí drew up a building with an almost symmetrical layout, in which two patios next to the entrance staircase and another two on the sides of the building allow sunlight to pour in.

The architect took great pains with the interior decoration of the apartments; he even designed some pieces of furniture, such as an armchair for one or two people, a table and a chair. This collection of furniture marked his first foray into the world of design.

Architect: Antoni Gaudí

Location: Carrer Casp, 48

Date: 1898-1900

See map 1

Casa Amatller

Josep Puig i Cadafalch was commissioned to refurbish a preexisting building typical of rented property, with the owner living in the main apartment on the first floor, and the other apartments rented out. The refurbishment retained only the inner structure and changed the entire façade. To do this, the architect drew on his knowledge of medieval art to create a work that combined elements from Dutch medieval architecture, such as the tiered crest, and Catalan medieval architecture, such as the third-floor gallery and the decoration on the ground floor and first story. This mixture of styles is complemented by decoration with sgraffito, wrought iron, ceramics and sculptures in stone and wood.

The ground floor is adorned with elements taken from the Catalan Gothic style, as was the device of setting sculpture around the openings but never on the walls or free-standing. The symmetrical design of the façade is only broken, very subtly, by the front door, which is set to one side. This leads on to one staircase that goes up to the heavily decorated main apartment and another that provides access to the other floors.

Architec: Josep Puig i Cadafalch

Location: Passeig de Gràcia, 41

Date: 1898-1900

See map 2

Casa Macaya

The house designed for the businessman Romà Macaya i Gibert followed the pattern for rented accommodation in the Eixample, with the first floor occupied by the owner's family and the remaining apartments rented out.

The irregular distribution of the openings on the façade recalls the Casa Amatller, built at the same time: there is a large stone balcony and gallery on the first floor, and windows that become smaller as the building gains height. The top of the house, with a gallery and two small turrets, is one of the many reinterpretations of Catalan civil Gothic architecture undertaken by Josep Puig i Cadafalch.

The central patio, which distributes the space and provides access to the first floor, is bigger than that of the Casa Amatller and other buildings designed by the same architect, partly due to the fact that the plot is wider than usual. The only technique used to decorate the walls of the patio and the façade is sgraffito against a white background; the ceramic tiles so common in the architect's other projects are absent here.

The building was recently converted into a cultural center, with much of the main apartment turned into a multi-media library, and despite the obvious modifications to the space great efforts were made to preserve all the decorative elements in the interior.

Architect: Josep Puig i Cadafalch

Location: Passeig de Sant Joan, 106

Date: 1899-1901

See map 2

Palau Burés

Francesc Burés i Borràs commissioned this sumptuous residential building from Miquel Pascual i Tintorer and made his home on the first floor; he rented out the rest of the apartments, in keeping with the typical model for rented blocks in the Eixample.

The four-story building has a façade of exposed stone, with large balconies on every floor and galleries on the first floor. The tiled roof projects out on to the street, leaving exposed thick wooden beams with sculptured heads of humanoids on the tips, evoking the Middle Ages. The turret on the corner of Carrer Girona is another element typical of this reworking of medieval features, while the corner of Carrer Ausiàs Marc is topped off with six pillars framing three windows—a much more modern approach than the copying of outdated medieval models. This building and its rich interior decoration—especially on the main staircase—illustrate the importance of Modernist trends in Barcelona.

Architect: Miquel Pascual i Tintorer

Location: Carrer Ausiàs Marc, 30-32

Date: 1900

See map 1

Casa Lleó Morera

This building, which received a prize from the Barcelona City Hall in 1905, corresponds to the pattern for rented property in the Eixample, with the owner living on the first story and running a business from the ground floor while renting out the remaining apartments. Lluís Domènech i Montaner used the area at the corner of the block as a key element that allowed him to spread the building over two symmetrical façades, joined by a narrow vertical strip set off by a small decorative dome and the gallery on the first floor.

The exposed stone accentuates the lines of the façade, with splashes of color only appearing on the dome and the ground floor. The architect managed to center all the decorative attention on the alternations in the various openings—which echo the interior layout—and their sculptural embellishments. As regards the ornamental elements on the façade, the round balconies on the second floor are typical of the time, as are the female figures bearing technological inventions of the period, such as the gramophone, telephone or light bulb.

Architect: Lluís Domènech i Montaner

Location: Passeig de Gràcia, 35

Date: 1905

See map 2

Bellesguard

The property's name, Bellesguard ("good view"), goes back to the 15th century, and refers to the location. When Antoni Gaudí accepted the commission little remained of the summer residence of King Martí I "L'Humà" that once stood here. What ruins there were have been left undisturbed.

The exterior, clad with natural, is reminiscent of medieval buildings and blends into its surroundings. The windows on the façade are lobed arches with a Gothic touch, and the tower flaunts one of Gaudí's most characteristic devices–the cross with four arms. The layout of the house is simple, virtually square, with a basement, ground floor, first story and attic. Low, paneled vaults supported by cylindrical pillars define the structure of the basement. In the main apartment above this, the brick vaults constitute a decorative ornament in their own right, but the most striking feature is the brightness, partly provided by large openings in the wall. On the upper floors Gaudí also flooded the rooms with light by inserting a large number of windows and covering the walls with plaster. The roof in the attic is supported by pillars in various shapes that are topped with mushroom-like brick protuberances.

Architect: Antoni Gaudí

Location: Carrer Bellesguard, 16-20

Date: 1900-1909

See map 3

Park Güell

Eusebi Güell had the new type of English garden city in mind when he decided to develop some land in the neighborhood of Gràcia. He gave the commission to his friend and protégé Antoni Gaudí with the aim of creating a residential space close to the city that would attract the Catalan upper-middle class, but in the end his initiative did not meet with the success that he had anticipated. Gaudí designed it as a residential complex, which is why the land had a boundary wall right from the start. Its wavy forms, set off by seven gates, were made with masonry edged with incrustations of ceramic fragments–a technique known as "trencadís". This ornamentation is repeated on several other elements. Opposite the entrance, a large double staircase leads to the Hipóstila Hall–made up of 86 classical columns–and the Greek theater–an esplanade above the hall, framed by a continuous, undulating bench. The two parts of the staircase are separated by small islands with organic elements: one in the form of a cave, one with a reptile's head emerging from a medallion with the Catalan flag and a third with the figure of a dragon.

Architect: Antoni Gaudí

Location: Carrer Olot, s/n.

Date: 1900-1914

See map 3

Casa Llopis Bofill

Antoni Moragas Gallisà collaborated with the architects Elies Rogent and Domènech i Montaner, because of his great ability to solve all types of decorative details by using craft techniques.

This building has several elements derived from Mozarab architecture, a style that was revived in Barcelona in the 1880s as a vernacular adaptation of the Orientalism that was sweeping Europe. The arches on the ground floor, with two distinct planes—the structural arches and the false tiered arches—are a response to this Orientalist trend, as is the profusion of glazed ceramics (although this technique already formed part of the tradition of the Iberian Levant). These possible stylistic allusions apart, the stretch of wall that dominates the entire building is finished with floral motifs traced on white plaster using sgraffito—a very common feature in Barcelona. The gallery hinted at on the top floor is a combination of a Mozarab idiom—glazed ceramics, stone and brick—with typical Catalan Gothic secular architecture. The pharmacy on the ground floor has retained its Modernist decoration and the glazed ceramic cladding on the curve under the arches has lost none of its charm.

Architect: Antoni Moragas Gallissà

Location: Carrer València, 339/Carrer Bailèn, 113

Date: 1902-1903

See map 2

Casa Martí

This building was one of the first in which Josep Puig i Cadafalch established a personal style that drew on his parallel training as a historian and architect. The interest in recovering Catalonia's medieval architectural heritage led him to incorporate a gallery on the top floor, as this was an element typical of the palaces and aristocratic houses of medieval Barcelona that was adopted by the architects of the late19th century. However, the other medieval-style elements are merely decorative and function independently of the wall, as simple additions to it. Without this decoration, the building would present an almost uninterrupted brick wall, vaguely reminiscent of the large blocks of walls without openings in southern Gothic architecture. The capacity to reinvent medieval elements distanced it from the more sterile architectural experiments being made at the time and looked forward to the concepts of Modernism.

This house, popularly known as Els Quatre Gats (the four cats) after the bar on its ground floor, was one of the focal points of fin-de-siècle modernity in Barcelona and showed work by artists like Ramon Casas, Santiago Rusiñol and Miquel Utrillo.

Architect: Josep Puig i Cadafalch

Location: Carrer Montsió, 3 bis

Date: 1895-1896

See map 1

Palau Quadras

This building currently provides an excellent home for the House of Asia. The project was the result of a thorough refurbishment of a preexisting home that was intended to be the residence of the Baron de Quadras. Lluís Puig i Cadafalch carried out other similar renovations at the end of the 19th century.

Taking the very narrow plot and the two façades as his starting point, the architect organized the house around a central patio, allowing some light to trickle into all the floors. The main façade is characterized by its broad gallery–profusely decorated with central European motifs–whose top section blends into the balustrade of the balcony on the second floor. The third level is realized by means of the classical continuous gallery, a feature recovered from the Catalan Gothic style. The ensemble is finished off with a tiled roof sloping toward the street, broken up by four exaggerated garrets that allow light into the attic. The rear façade was approached more simply, with slatted blinds. The outstanding elements inside are the magnificent fireplace on the first floor and the ceramic tiles that line the entrance.

Architect: Lluís Puig i Cadafalch

Location: Avinguda Diagonal, 373

Date: 1899-1906

See map 2

Casa Larribal

Pere Falquès es an architect who is difficult to classify on account of the freedom with which he used elements of the classical idiom and other sources; a good illustration of this is provided by this distinctive building in the old town, which mixes this eclecticism with touches of Modernism.

The building is set on a corner plot in Carrer Avinyó, which was very popular with the upper-middle class at the time. As it was surrounded by narrow streets, the architect decided to relinquish space on the corner and set the façade back from the road, thereby gaining visual impact.

The decoration is focused on the corner façade, with a frenetic rhythm and a series of classical elements deformed to previously unimaginable extremes, such as the two squat pillars on the first floor, which are seemingly flattened by the triumphal arch on the second floor. Similarly, the five pillars on the third floor do not rest on the top of the arch but emerge much higher up out of the wall itself.

Architect: Pere Falqués i Urpí

Location: Carrer Avinyó, 13

Date: 1902

See map 1

Hospital de la Santa Creu and Sant Pau

The Hospital de Sant Pau was created as the new health center for the city, to replace the Hospital de Santa Creu, the Gothic building in Carrer Hospital that currently houses the National Library of Catalonia. Spread over an entire large block, the complex designed by Lluís Domènech i Montaner recreates the idea of a city, with separate buildings and efficient connections between the various functions—accesses, wards, consulting rooms, kitchens—that were highly unusual and progressive in the context of hospital planning at that time. Despite the constant refurbishments that have been undertaken to improve the hospital services, the complex remains a landmark of Modernisme and displays an evident interest in city planning. Particularly striking are the duplication of the buildings designed for the various medical specialties, with their distinctive asymmetry, and the masterly use of brick as a basic building material, applied with a number of techniques. Also worthy of note is the decorative work, largely designed by Pau Gargallo, a sculptor who had already collaborated with the architect on the Palau de la Música.

Architects: Lluís Domènech i Montaner and Víctor Argentí

Location: Carrer Sant Antoni Maria Claret, 171

Date: 1902-1911 and 1913-1930

See map 2

Casa Terrades

Josep Puig i Cadafalch designed several homes in a single unit to fill an irregularly shaped plot between Avinguda Diagonal and Carrer Rosselló in the Eixample. The building is commonly known as the Casa de les Punxes (house of thorns), after the iron tips on the roofs and towers. It is equipped with three staircases and boasts a bay that runs right round the perimeter of the block—a space with two load-bearing walls—and turrets on the corners, which add definition and unity to the diffuse layout of the building. The turret on the main corner is particularly striking as it is higher and more ornamental than the others. All the walls follow the same pattern—a gallery on the first three floors, a balcony on the fourth and a window on the top story—thereby bestowing unity on all the façades, even though they are of different sizes; the elements on the roofs are also repeated, although with slight modifications.

The Central European Gothic repertoire that was always dear to this architect's heart is present in almost all the elements of the building, from the turrets and the continuous double slope of the roofs to the array of decorative elements. However, the use of craft techniques typical of Modernism in the ornamentation and the rationality with which the project was realized distance the building from Neo-Gothic concepts and place it within the mainstream of Modernism.

Architect: Josep Puig i Cadafalch

Location: Avinguda Diagonal, 416-420/ Carrer Rosselló, 260-262

Date: 1903-1905

See map 2

Casa Roviralta

This house, built by the Roviralta family, formed part of the garden city promoted and laid out lengthwise along the road by the Tibidabo Company.

Popularly known as the Frare blanc (the white friar), as the land belonged to the Dominicans, this building is one of the most representative examples of the architect's Modernist phase. He exalted and exaggerated the typical elements of Catalan architecture, such as the large open garret and the use of rough brickwork, and took the latter to its decorative limits on the eaves. The L-shape layout contains one main quadrangular block with stairs in the center that serve as the axis connecting all the spaces. The fact that the architect did not strive for perpendicularity in the other block but adapted it to the terrain and sunlight are indicative of a greater freedom; similarly, the large sitting room on the first floor has a very irregular shape.

The use of white stucco, which was somewhat unusual at the time, sets off the brickwork, not only on the building but also on the boundary wall.

Architect: Joan Rubió i Bellver

Location: Avinguda Tibidabo, 31

Date: 1903-1913

See map 3

This and the other buildings in the old citadel are examples of the French-style Neoclassicism introduced into the city's architecture after the triumph of the House of Borbón in the War of Succession (1708-1714).

The Arsenal of the old military citadel consisted of two naves laid out in the shape of a cross, with four patios in its crosspieces that give the building a square structure. The main façade of the parade ground fronted a block of similar dimensions to the interlocked naves, and its various rooms served to store weapons; it was enlarged for the first time in 1919 by Pere Falqués to create a royal palace by turning the simple structure into a more luxurious building. In 1932, after further refurbishments, it was converted into the house of the Parliament of Catalonia, not only for pragmatic reasons but also because of its symbolism, as the building had been the center of the military repression that Catalonia experienced after 1714. Under Franco's dictatorship a museum was installed inside, but the complex has now reverted to its function as the Parliament building.

Architect: Jorge Próspero de Verboom

Location: Parc de la Ciutadella, s/n.

Date: 1716-1727

See map 1

Casa Batlló

Pere Milà, a fervent admirer of Gaudí and friend of the textile manufacturer Josep Batlló, did not hesitate to introduce the two men when he learnt of the latter's intention to modernize his home. The Casa Batlló had been standing since 1877 when its owner commissioned Gaudí to refurbish the façade and redistribute the wells of the building. Even though Gaudí was dealing with a preexisting construction, he succeeded in bestowing a highly personal touch on the project–so much so that this house became one of the most emblematic works of his long career. His compositional sensitivity is immediately apparent from the exterior, which is covered with Marés stone and glass on the lower floors and ceramic discs on the upper ones. During the construction work Gaudí stood in the street and personally chose the best positions for these pieces in order to make them stand out and gleam, and the workers gradually put them in place. This approach to his work–the perfecting of an initial idea during the building process –reflects the great dedication Gaudí brought to his projects, which he almost never considered to be finished. This method caused him some bureaucratic problems, as the authorities needed to approve complete projects.

Architect: Antoni Gaudí

Location: Passeig de Gràcia, 43

Date: 1904-1906

See map 2

Palau de la Música Catalana

Lluís Domènech i Montaner created one of the most emblematic Modernista buildings–and one of the most loved by Barcelona's citizens–with his project for the concert hall and headquarters of the Orfeó Català. Set on an irregular plot in the old town, the building is organized around the auditorium, which is its key element. For the ceiling of this large concert hall, the architect used a weight-bearing structure made with a metal frame–a technique he rarely used, but in this case it provided him with a simple means of spanning a large space. The idea of spatial continuation dominates the interior: the entrance and the staircase run uninterrupted right up to the doors leading into the hall. Inside, the applied arts take pride of place by enveloping the entire surface of the auditorium, with the large inverted cupola as the crowning point. The façade is built of solid brick, with fretwork on both the large balconies supported by single pillars and the much more subtle tracery on the side wall; as a result the static mass of brick vibrates with an interplay between solid volumes and hollows that is set off by the multi-colored decoration of the arches and pillars that mark the openings.

Architect: Lluís Domènech i Montaner

Location: Carrer Amadeu Vives, 1

Date: 1909

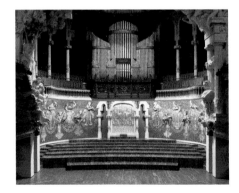

See map 1

Casa Milà

The Casa Milà—also known as the Pedrera (quarry) on account of its resemblance to a large rock formation—was commissioned by Pere Milà and his wife as a home with additional apartments to let. It was the last civil building designed by Antoni Gaudí, as he then went on to immerse himself in his work on the Sagrada Família.

Gaudí came up with a method for saving materials that he used to create a building that was unprecedented in the Western architectural traditions of the time. He substituted load-bearing walls with a system of summers and pillars, and he took meticulous care with the joins in order to be able to reduce the walls' dimensions. In this way he not only managed to mold the façade to his fancy but also laid out the inner spaces as he saw fit—thereby creating the first open-plan floor space in the history of modern architecture. Although the façade looks robust, it is in fact made up of thin sheets of limestone with a self-supporting structure. Other outstanding features are the two inner wells, the garage in the basement, with a ramp, and the magnificent terrace with its views of the city.

In 1886 the building underwent a refurbishment that eliminated the apartments put into the garret by Francisco J. Barba Corsini in 1954, which had made it possible to establish an in situ correlation with the first fifty years of modern architecture. However, this intervention exposed the parabolic arches, revealing one of the best spaces in which to understand the architecture of Gaudí, and the adjoining terrace, one of Barcelona's most beautiful vantage points.

Architect: Antoni Gaudí

Location: Passeig de Gràcia, 92

Date: 1905-1910

See map 2

Casa Comalat

This residential building set between party walls was put up on a block somewhat that is unusual for the Eixample, as Cerdà's typical block is reduced to a third of its size on account of the Avinguda Diagonal, and as a result it loses the characteristic large inner patio. The main façade and the entrances are situated on the Diagonal, but their design is somewhat rigid in comparison to the imaginative devices of the great Modernista architects, and the only expressive touches are the treatment of the ground floor and the cupola on the top. In contrast, the façade on Carrer Còrsega succeeds in capturing the architect's personal style, with an interplay of dynamic forms that is now much admired, although at the time this rear part of the building was dismissed as little more than an afterthought compared to the front.

Furthermore, the back of the building is situated on the corner of the block—although it does not occupy it in its entirety—and this does not allow for any symmetry between its two stretches of wall. Instead of trying to hide this irregularity, the architect emphasized it with the rounded forms of the galleries on the first two floors, and with the use of different designs on each wall for the galleries on the top two floors.

Architect: Salvador Valeri i Pupurull

Location: Avinguda Diagonal, 442/
Carrer Còrsega, 316

Date: 1909-1911

See map 2

Fábrica Casaramona

This late example of Catalan Modernism is far removed from the historicism and revision of medieval architecture to which Josep Puig i Cadafalch was so devoted, although paradoxically it his most personal project.

The rationalization required to create a manufacturing space on an almost square plot led to a simple program and the use of a cheap building material: brick. Two inner alleyways divide the overall space into three distinct blocks: two large halls at either ends, and another hall with offices in the central area.

Its light structure made it possible to restore it and create a spacious basement ex novo to serve its new function as a cultural center. To avoid modifying the original walls, Arata Isozaki, who was responsible for the conversion, designed a direct entrance to this basement, which is linked to the interior of the factory by means of a large glass-and-iron pergola, which contrasts with the old construction and establishes itself as a separate form.

Although its dimensions are smaller than those of the block designed by Cerdà—already drawn up in Pere García Fària's 1891 map for the north part of Poble Sec and the area of the Plaça de Espanya—the building reflects its layout and adapts to the mountainous terrain. Its relationship to the layout of the Eixample is clear, although it is now isolated from it by the other buildings around it.

Architect: Josep Puig i Cadafalch

Location: Carrer Mèxic, 36-44

Date: 1910-1911

See map 1

Plaza de toros Monumental

Spanish bullrings have failed to give rise to a particular architectural idiom; instead, they have generally drawn on an eclectic style with obvious Neo-Arab and Neo-Mudejar influences. This is partly explained by the fact that guidelines for the construction of bullrings were never established because they were originally temporary, purely functional wooden structures that only became permanent venues over the course of time. At the beginning of the 19th century Barcelona had only one bullring, in Barceloneta, which, despite its considerable size, was a temporary construction. It no longer exists, and is mainly known through various late-19th-century paintings, particularly some by Marià Fortuny.

The bullring is incorporated into a block in the Eixample, with the main entrance at the junction of Carrer Marina and Gran Via, the northern side facing the stables and the western face giving on to some small outhouses, which currently contain a small museum.

Architect: Ignasi Mas i Martorell

Location: Gran Via de les Corts Catalanes/
Carrer Marina

Date: 1913-1915

See map 1

Estació de França

The Estació de França is a typical example of a 19th-century railroad station, although it is distinguished by the sinuous curve traced by the platforms, which obliges the arches overhead to follow the same movement. The 1925 project replaced the smaller station that had stood on this spot since 1848, marking the terminus of the oldest railroad track in Spain. The original station was built beside the old military citadel and so was adapted to the terrain by creating a slight curve, which can still be found not only in the present building but also in the streets around the station and in the Parc de la Ciutadella. The track acted as an architectural barrier between the neighborhood of Poble Nou and the rest of the city that only lost its significance in the run-up to the Olympic Games in 1992.

This extensive complex is outstanding for its entrance hall, with decoration influenced by Catalan Noucentisme, and the glass canopies overlooking the street. Some of its premises are currently occupied by the Pompeu Fabra University. When seen from the ring road the building's structure looks like a blemish on the urban fabric, isolating Barceloneta and the sea from this part of the city.

Architect: Pedro de Muguruza

Location: Avinguda Marquès de l'Argentera, s/n.

Date 1925-1930

See map 1

Casa Masana

This housing complex marked one the first attempts in Spain to build affordable homes on a mass scale in accordance with the advanced ideas then prevailing in central European architecture.

The construction process was rationalized to build these blocks: a mass production of elements to reduce the construction schedule and the use of cheap, modern materials. The architect set the apartments along the outside of the building to make the most of the direct ventilation from the street. There is no large inner patio, and so he could also put the staircase on the façade; this is open to view as a result of the V-shape window screening it, which sheds light on the interior as well as setting the rhythm of the façade and indicating the entrance to each apartment block. The use of this expressive device to satisfy a functional requirement is one of the visual characteristics that clearly reflects the architect's interest in the concepts that were being developed in Germany and Holland, especially within the circles of the Bauhaus.

However, this experiment proved insufficient for absorbing the immigrants that arrived in Barcelona at the end of the 1920s as a result of the demand for labor for the Universal Exhibition in 1929.

Architect: Ramón Raventós i Farrarons

Location: Carrer Lleida, 9-10

Date: 1928

See map 1

Fábrica Myrurgia

This old perfume factory fits into the layout of Cerdà's Eixample, occupying a third of one of its blocks.

The building contained both the factory floor and some small offices, and each use was reflected by a different treatment on the façade. The corner of Carrer Mallorca provided access to the offices, so it is higher and has bas-reliefs on the thresholds of the doors; in contrast, the corner on Carrer Provença was given just one large door, as the entrance had direct access on to the factory and the bays for loading and unloading trucks. While the factory is designed along strictly functional lines–closely following the modern principles of mass production and lighting from large windows–the office section is a combination of traditional ideas and modern forms.

The symmetry of the façade, the bas-reliefs and the importance of the large lobby with the main staircase are elements that are clearly indebted to a classical conception of architecture, while the continuous windows, the metal structure exposed to view and the use of mass-produced materials respond to a more avant-garde European aesthetic.

Architect: Antoni Puig Gairalt

Location: Carrer Mallorca, 315

Date: 1928-1930

See map 2

Palau Nacional

The current home of the National Museum of the Art of Catalonia (MNAC) on the Montjuïc mountain was the main building put up for the Universal Exhibition in 1929. It is characterized by an unimaginative eclecticism, as the large cupola is an imitation of that of Saint Peter's, while the side towers clumsily copy the Giralda. The original project was drawn up by Lluís Puig i Cadafalch, but it was realized by several architects who did not share the same cultural viewpoint as this Catalan artist and politician. Apart from the monotonous use of the classical order–diffuse and disproportionate, with elements juxtaposed without any relationship–the most striking feature is the oval hall, which at the time was the largest covered space without pillars in the whole of Europe. The 1980s saw the start of costly refurbishment works, supervised by Gae Aulenti, who had previously been responsible for the Orsay Museum. The intention was to turn the building into a museum. New foundations were laid, as the temporary nature of the construction meant that neither the materials nor the structure had been designed to last. The idea was to create a museum along the lines of the great French institutions, but this has failed to materialize as the museum has never succeeded in becoming an integral part of the city.

The outline of the palace has become one of Barcelona's distinctive landmarks, and since 1962 it has been classified as a Monument of National Interest.

Architects: Enric Català i Català and Pedro Cendoya Oscoz

Location: Plaça del Mirador, s/n.

Date: 1925-1929

See map 1

German Pavilion

Mies van der Rohe devoted much time in obstinately–and apparently incomprehensibly–changing the placement of the building he wanted to put up. The spot he chose lies on the route that the public had to take from the entrance to the exhibition's grounds on the way up to the Poble Espanyol. This setting allows the pavilion to display its entire length as a subtle barrier on this route, as a beautiful foreign body designed for contemplation while also reflecting the image of its surroundings with a delicate interplay of glass that acts like a mirror.

The idea of the path–inherited from Karl Friedrich Schinkel–is discreetly repeated in the interior, with its suggestion of the start of a maze. The architecture is formally defined as a conjunction of horizontal and vertical planes that serves both for a pavilion and a home. The pool (which originally boasted water lilies) and the small side element balance the composition of the main volume; both these forms are mounted on a base measuring 174 x 56 ft. Indoors, another pool with a statue repeats the exterior composition.

Architect: Ludwig Mies van der Rohe.
Reconstruction by Manuel Solà-Morales, Cristian Cirici y Fernando Ramos

Location: Avinguda del Marquès de Comillas, s/n.

Date: 1929. Reconstruction: 1986

See map 1

Casal Sant Jordi

This block was originally designed to contain a combination of offices and homes, but in the 1980s it was converted into the premises of the Ministry of Justice of the Generalitat.

The building, dominated by strong, straight lines, occupies a corner of a block in Barcelona's Eixample, and it is higher than any of its neighbors. The façade displays a clear central European inspiration as it reflects the concepts of the Moderne Bauformen. The openings are larger on the upper stories; this distinction formerly marked out the different functions of the building. A large podium comprising a ground floor and a first story endowed with smooth, austere walls gives way to three floors of offices with a series of windows set off by protuberances in the façade that create six unusual galleries. On the upper stories, which were given over to the residences, the windows are repeated in the galleries and on the edges of the building, leaving large areas of the wall unbroken. The difference in the size of the windows emphasizes the contrast between the full and empty spaces. The top floor has few openings and also lacks the galleries; its proportions are similar to the podium at the base of the building.

Architect: Francesc Folguera i Grassi

Location: Carrer Pau Claris, 81

Date: 1929-1931

See map 1

Housing on Via Augusta

This building finds a simple way to accommodate a scheme of two large homes per floor, with the elevator shaft and the staircase in the middle of the block and two small wells that are shared with the adjacent buildings.

Despite the fact that the elements on the façade are not symmetrical, the architect played with a layout of the openings that is easily visible thanks to an axis of symmetry: the central part of the building is unbroken, while two rows of balconies flanked by two windows are set on either side, reflecting the internal arrangement of the block. The ground floor follows this pattern, with two large openings with enclosures set back slightly from the plane of the façade. This device succeeds in reducing the impact of the visual differences between the two; although they are both intended as commercial premises, the opening on the left also contains the building's main entrance, while the other is divided in two by a large pillar. This supporting pillar is absolutely essential as it connected to the load-bearing wall of the façade (which also explains why there are less windows and balconies on this side).

Architect: Germán Rodríguez Arias

Location: Via Augusta, 61

Date: 1930-1931

See map 2

Housing on Carrer Muntaner

This building, one of the earliest works of Josep Lluís Sert, is an example of one of the two types of housing that particularly concerned the modern movement: on the one hand, cheap, functional but high-quality homes for workers, such as the Casa Bloc; on the other, spacious homes for wealthy families, such as this block, which reinvents the concepts of luxury and comfort, just as Le Corbusier did in his villas.

The project involved six homes, each spread over two floors, and a spacious studio with a terrace on the top story, which went to the architect himself. The interior layout of the duplex homes is visible from the exterior, as the façade alternates two different types of opening, following a functional logic.

The use of tubular steel for the handrails, the construction of small corner balconies and the addition of glass panels illustrate Sert's desire to take advantage of the most rational elements of the modern idiom, in line with the teachings of his master, Le Corbusier.

Architect: Josep Lluís Sert

Location: Carrer Muntaner, 342

Date: 1930-1931

See map 2

Housing block

This project was quite innovative at a time when Noucentism was the prevailing esthetic trend in the city and the more modern ideas of the GATCPAC were still little known.

Apart from the volumetric interplay on the façade and some echoes of Art Deco, the building provides evidence of a particular interest in rationalist architecture and the social and technical advances of the time. It included a parking lot with access to the residents' staircase—a feature that was then almost unheard of—and the layout of the apartments is meticulously planned, with well-defined convenient interior spaces that are not subordinated to the forms of the façade. Moreover, the use of stiff blinds and the concern to create terraces or spacious balconies for most of the homes reveal a desire to take advantage of Barcelona's sunny weather.

The block has some features that draw on the experiments conducted in Central Europe such as the superimposition of various volumes on the façade and the continuous balconies with tubular handrails.

Architect: Carles Martínez i Sánchez

Location: Via Augusta, 12

Date: 1932

See map 2

Casa Bloc

This building formed part of a project for the mass construction of cheap housing which the Generalitat entrusted the GATCPAC to improve the living conditions of the more disadvantaged social classes.

The block was defined in the form of a large S, with two expansive public patios, and it was ideally placed in terms of sunlight and ventilation. The homes are reached via corridors running along the façade; they are spread over two levels, with an entrance on the lower one, which is also where the daytime activities are concentrated. The residential buildings occupy two blocks and try to adapt Le Corbusier's ideas about "immeubles-villes"–large buildings with all the facilities of a small town–to the reality of the urban layout. The project was rounded off by the construction of service facilities–nursery schools, baths, a cooperative and a social club–and the experiment was due to be repeated, but the Spanish Civil War and the subsequent victory of the rebel forces put an end to any such new developments. After the war the building went on to house policemen's families; its structure was changed by the addition of another block, which closed off one of the large patios and modified its characteristic "S" shape.

Architect: Josep Lluís Sert

Location: Passeig de Torras i Bages, 91-105

Date: 1932-1936

See map 2

Roca jewelry store

Josep Lluís Sert refurbished the ground floor of an existing building to house the Roca jewelry store, which was one of the city's most famous establishments at that time. Sert sought to bestow sobriety both inside and outside with a combination of sophisticated materials—marble and hard stones—and much cheaper mass-produced elements. He did not take into account the symmetry of the store, which is set on a corner, as discreetly tucked the entrance into one end and made the large windows the focus of attention. These have panels set behind the jewelry on display so that the interior cannot be seen from the street, in order to protect the privacy of the customers. This device had the disadvantage of blocking the light coming through the windows, so a long strip of glass bricks was put in above them by way of compensation, thereby also creating uniformity and sobriety. Another interesting feature of the façade is its form, which is reminiscent of a ship.

This commission is an example of the acceptance of the modern idiom by high society, and like them it complemented other projects that explored structural innovations and social concerns.

Architect: Josep Lluís Sert

Location: Passeig de Gràcia, 18

Date: 1934

See map 1

Anti-tuberculosis Dispensary

This building comprises three blocks laid out in a U shape around a patio, with the entrance facing east. At one end stands the caretaker's house, perched on piles; it has now been converted into a small museum. The other two blocks, both with three stories, are linked to form an L shape; the longer wing is given over to medical care, while the shorter contains the administration and, on the ground floor, a spacious conference room. The staircases and elevators are set in the corners of the blocks—on the vertex of the L and at its two ends.

The façades, with light aluminum cladding, alternate large windows with stretches of wall interrupted only by small high windows, which give continuity to the inner passageway running alongside the patio. The façade designed by Torres i Amat is fitted with continuous windows, except for one section on the second floor occupied by the X-ray room. The large solarium on the roof is protected from the wind by high walls.

This is one of the GATCPAC's most paradigmatic buildings. It is currently a Social Security clinic, and it still retains some of its original furnishings.

Architects: Josep Lluís Sert, Josep Torres and Joan Subirana

Location: Passatge de Sant Bernat, 10

Date: 1934-1938

See map 1

Barraquer Clinic

This building houses one of the most prestigious ophthalmologic clinics in the world. Although the project was launched in the period of the greatest fervor of the GATCPAC, Joaquim Lloret i Homs intentionally distanced himself from this tendency and drew on the Central European models of the 1930s, while also borrowing elements from Art Deco, such as the lavish attention paid to the interiors, in keeping with a rich private clinic.

The building is set on a corner but avoids a right angle by blending the two faces into a gentle curve and places the emphasis on volume. The dominant element is the continuous strips of windows, which mark out a strong horizontal motif that is only interrupted by the exposed metal girders, which act as a vertical counterpoint. The horizontality is further stressed by the base, which adapts to the slope of the terrain; it is finished with the same dark stone as the subtle cornice that tops the building and marks the end of the girders. The main entrance is characterized by the use of the same material as the base and by its slight protuberance from the rest of the wall. A convex tube of dark glass, housing the main staircase, similarly juts out; it goes up to the roof terrace and allows light to flood into the staircase, as well as emphasizing the main entrance.

The refurbishments that have been subsequently carried out on the building have preserved the elegance and functionality of the original design.

Architect: Joaquim Lloret i Homs

Location: Carrer Muntaner, 314

Date: 1934-1940

See map 2

Spanish Republic Pavilion

In 1937 Spain took part in the International Exhibition in Paris in an attempt to raise awareness about the Republican cause in the international community. The pavilion was commissioned from Josep Lluís Sert and Luis Lacasa, and it had to adjust to the regulations of the Parisian municipal corporation; prominent among these was the ban on the uprooting of any trees—so the back staircase leading to the second floor traces an unusual curve to avoid a tree.

Sert, who had designed a portable art gallery to mount touring exhibitions for the GATCPAC, decided to display not only works by famous artists (Pablo Picasso, Joan Miró, Juan Gil Alberto, Juli González, Alexander Calder) but also a sample of popular crafts and some informative panels explaining the achievements of the Republic and the situation in the war.

Sert and Lacasa came up with a three-story building. They left the bottom level open and linked it to the patio covered by a canvas that served as a theater. The two upper floors are reached by the staircase that goes up to the first story and a ramp leading to the second; there was also a vertical entrance in the interior of the structure.

The pavilion was destroyed once the exhibition was over, and in the process a painting by Miró, "The Reaper", was lost. In 1992 it was decided to rebuild the pavilion in Barcelona; it currently houses a center containing documentation from the Spanish Civil War.

Architects: Josep Lluís Sert and Luis Lacasa. Rebuilt by Miquel Espinet, Antoni Ubach and José Miguel Hernandez León

Location: Carrer Jorge Manrique, s/n.

Date: 1937. Reconstruction: 1992

See map 3

Park Hotel

This hotel was one of the first buildings put up in the period after the Spanish Civil War that attempted to restore the link with modern trends. Antoni Moragas always had the intention—in both his architectural work and his intense cultural activism—to restore the city's modern character and integrate it into the movements and debates that had taken root in Europe. He was one of the prime movers of the Group R, and the organizer of the lecture given by Bruno Zevi in the Architects' Association in 1951, when Barcelona was still in the grip of the post-war atmosphere.

The building occupies a long, narrow block. The main façade was very small and, to give it a greater impact, it was conceived as a projection, with long balconies that opened out on the sides and were divided into two by a discreet, perforated sheet of concrete. This vertical element sets off the balconies and makes them appear much wider.

The question of accommodating the 100 planned hotel rooms was resolved on a rational basis. A large central corridor was designed with rooms on both sides, all with windows. The form of the building fits quite well into its urban context, despite the fact that this largely consists of 19th-century buildings set out on a partly medieval layout.

The bar on the ground floor, which has recently been restored, is a good example of meticulous care in industrial design—a characteristic that also came to be associated with Moragas.

Architects: Antoni Moragas Gallissà and Francesc Riba i Salas

Location: Avinguda Marqués de l'Argentera, 11

Date: 1950-1954

See map 1

Casa de la Marina

This small building, designed to provide cheap apartments, is one of the most emblematic works of José Antonio Coderch's early phase, in which he mixed elements taken from popular architecture with a modern program.

Although the plot is almost square, Coderch drew up the layout of the homes without any walls at right angles, to avoid any dead areas and take the fullest advantage of the space. This approach is reflected on the exterior by the slight movement on two of the three façades, which makes the building stand out within the regular configuration of the Barceloneta neighborhood. However, this effect is counterbalanced in its turn by the base—a double-height volume with walls at 90-degree—and the large, similarly quadrangular canopy that tops off the building and subtly integrates it into its surroundings.

The use of slatted blinds and orange ceramic tiles on the façade and self-supporting walls in the small inner patio and stairwell marked an updating of these elements and construction forms and proved that the popular tradition was not at odds with modernity. Architects from both home and abroad recognized the excellence of this building, which was created during a critical period for the basic premises of modern architecture, as these were being subject to review and vernacular architecture was experiencing a revival.

Architect: José Antonio Coderch de Sentmenat

Location: Passeig Joan de Borbó / Comte de Barcelona, 43

Date: 1952-1953

See map 1

Eucharistic Congress housing project

In the context of insufficient housing to absorb the constant influx of immigrants, the Eucharistic Congress held in Barcelona proved an appropriate event for creating a low-rent residential complex.

This project, one of the city's first housing estates, involved the construction of 3,000 public-housing apartments, 300 commercial premises and a church. It comprised two types of blocks, some rectangular, the others higher, cross-shaped and extremely functional, despite their symbolic form, which was chosen to commemorate the Congress. These two kinds of blocks stretch out along the two sides of a rectangular square; one of the shorter sides is traced by the busy Carrer Felip II, while the other contains the imposing church, which dominates the ensemble.

Despite the fact that this residential estate was built in a far-flung and poorly communicated corner of the city, with serious planning deficiencies, nowadays it has become an integral part of Barcelona.

Architects: Carles Marquès, Antoni Pineda and Josep Soteras

Location: Plaça del Congrés Eucarístic, s/n.

Fecha: 1952-1961

See map 3

Luminor Building

The inclusion of office buildings in the city's historic quarter reflects the series of sometimes erratic attempts at urban renewal that emerged in the 1950s, when the economy was still faltering.

This building with an L-shape layout stands out as an isolated and conspicuous form in the surrounding urban fabric, but its construction did make it possible to open up the Plaça de Castella–an area where space was in short supply–and put in an underground parking lot.

The ground floor is clad with dark stone, but the remainder of the building uses a variety of pale-colored materials, which add a touch of lightness. The enclosure of the first floor protrudes slightly from the façade, almost like a gallery; the other three floors are given over to windows, with a configuration that matches that of the stanchions. These vertical supports are set inside the first-floor gallery, barely 18 inches from the glass, and this simple resource manages to bestow personality on what would otherwise be an anonymous concrete façade. The canopy on the top floor is another distinctive feature, and its curved edges provide relief from the austerity of the rest of the building.

Architects: Josep Soteras and José Antonio
Coderch de Sentmenat

Location: Plaça de Castella

Date: 1953-1955. Extension: 1961

See map 1

Gustavo Gili publishing house

The building for the headquarters of this emblematic Barcelona publishing house sought to recover the basic tenets of the modern movement, even though by the 1950s these were beginning to be questioned in many countries. The architects especially wanted to throw light on the contribution of the GATCPAC, with which Joaquim Gili had collaborated when he was a student. One of the ideas that this modern local group proposed, but never put into practice, was the use of the patios in the blocks of Cerdà's Eixample for tertiary purposes, in an attempt to mix residential functions with services and offices. This idea, which is still alive today, led the architects to build the publishing house's headquarters in the patio of a block in the Eixample.

The interior of the block is reached by a passageway with a paved pedestrian entrance. Inside the large patio, the three low sections of the building—management, offices and warehouse—are spread round a small square with a garden, leaving some of the space unoccupied. The main section, given over to the offices, is perhaps the most emblematic element, with a sobriety in keeping with the best of the modern school; its most striking feature is the projecting, slatted, double-height "blind", which allows light to enter the large entrance lobby.

Architects: Francesc Bassó and Joaquim Gili

Location: Carrer Rosselló, 89

Date: 1954-1961

See map 2

Montbau housing estate

This estate was largely designed as an open unit that permitted the addition of new elements. The complex was built in three phases, which meant that it could be adjusted to requirements more gradually than other estates, although in the early years it did share many of their problems: appalling infrastructures, isolation and a lack of shopping facilities. The first building phase focussed on the sector with linear blocks lining the squares, which went on to mark the construction scheme for the entire area. A subsequent phase saw the construction of the large square buildings, which have become reference points, as they can be seen from the Ronda de Dalt.

The pattern of squares and large blocks was laid out with a number of streets, which were later linked to new buildings, allowing the estate to blend into its surroundings.

The apartments in the rectangular blocks are spread over two floors, with views from both sides; this arrangement was made possible by placing the load-bearing walls perpendicular to the façade.

Architects: Guillermo Giráldez, Pedro López, Ignacio Xavier Subías, Manuel Baldrich, Antoni Bonet and Josep Soteras

Location: Passeig de la Vall d'Hebrón, s/n.

Date: 1957-1965

See map 3

This building is an example of the recovery of the modern research that was interrupted by the Spanish Civil War. Even though its architects copied the ideas of the architectural movement of the 1930s, they had a distinctive outlook. As a result, the building stood apart and other works aroused greater interest at the time–for example, the Seat plant, built by César Ortiz.

This essentially functional building has two very distinct areas: the four-story tower and the adjacent low building; the former contains the classrooms and the study areas, while the latter houses both the conference room and the administrative offices within its two parallel, independent elements (connected to the administration area by an expansive lobby), each with three inner patios and two stories.

All the materials used in the building are the derived from industrial production, from the iron girders to the tiles and the prefabricated concrete walls with windows in standard sizes.

Architects: Guillermo Giráldez, Pedro López and Ignacio Xavier Subías

Location: Avinguda Diagonal, 684

Date: 1958-1959

See map 3

Headquarters of the COAC

The headquarters of COAC (Official Architects' Association of Catalonia) are located in a building near the Cathedral. Although the building's office block is obviously indebted to modern postulates and architectural language, the lower section, containing the reception, gallery and lecture room, responds more closely to the ideas of the 1950s, in a clear attempt to blend in with its surroundings. So, while the block soars up as an isolated element indifferent to the reality of the setting, the lower form strives to be permeable and adapts to the layout of the medieval street, but this contrast does not create a clash. On the contrary, both sections combine to form a whole that has become one of Barcelona's emblematic landmarks.

The eight-floor office block displays a very simple, clear and regulated façade: similarly proportioned horizontal lines made of concrete and glass succeed each other vertically, while six iron girders, spaced out equidistantly, are left exposed on the face of the building. Each of these intervals is, in its turn, set off by three mullions that support the cladding of cement slabs and glass.

The front section is intended to remain open to the street, and so the ground floor is lined with glass, although the story above is covered with large, unbroken panels with sgraffitos of drawings by Pablo Picasso, undertaken specially for the building. The lecture room boasts another drawing by the same artist.

Architect: Xavier Busquets

Location: Carrer Arcs, 1

Date: 1958-1962

See map 1

Antoni Tàpies' house-workshop

This house, belonging to the painter Antoni Tàpies, is situated in the former town of Sant Gervasi (now incorporated into the city limits); it occupies a long, narrow plot typical of the towns on the Barcelona plain, and this configuration has a decisive effect on the character of the building.

The front part of the ground floor houses the domestic staff, while the rear is taken up by the artist's large double-height studio, fitted with skylights that distribute the sunlight evenly throughout the space.

The main focus does not fall on the façade, as the block receives more sunshine to the rear and is lit and ventilated by two inner patios.

The living area is spread over the three upper floors, which are only constructed in the front section, as the building regulations do not permit construction to this height over the entire surface area of such deep plots. The building's highly unassuming façade is conceived as a uniform expanse, with even the access virtually indistinguishable. The ground floor is dominated by the brown of the simple main entrance and garage door, which are set next to a brick wall. The other floors are finished with fixed, slatted blinds, which give the façade a hermetic, uniform look.

Architect: José Antonio Coderch de Sentmenat

Location: Carrer Saragossa, 57

Date: 1960-1963

See map 2

Mitre Building

The Mitre Building, an 11-story low-rent block with seven independent access staircases, contains 298 apartments of various sizes. The project aimed to create a self-sufficient housing unit with service facilities—ranging from a laundromat to a pharmacy—on the ground floor, following the pattern that was emerging at that time in Europe.

The 276 smaller apartments, measuring 495 sq. ft, are fairly flexible, with sliding doors and the possibility of changing the layout, thanks to the fact that the structural walls perpendicular to the façade are the only ones that separate the homes. Another dynamic element is the bathroom with two doors, allowing access from both the main bedroom and the small corridor. Although the homes are small and are all built along the same lines, they are of high quality and display excellent finishing, such as the balconies made with masonry, calculated to be sufficiently opaque to preserve the intimacy of the occupants while allowing an optimum illumination of their homes.

Architect: Francisco J. Barba Corsini

Location: Ronda General Mitre, 1-13

Date: 1960-1963

See map 3

Casa Meridiana

This building was commissioned as a block of 121 small homes, on a somewhat inflexible plot that was unfavorably orientated. The project was an attempt to adapt Mediterranean architectural traditions to the taxing building conditions of mass housing.

The center of the large rectangular block is broken up by four spacious patios that provide the apartments with light and ventilation. Three stairwells and elevator shafts are situated on this central axis, while the apartments are lined up along both façades. The windows jut out from the façade to create small galleries that are open to the south but closed to the north, in order to improve the apartments' natural lighting while maintaining their privacy. Similarly, two distinct modules of openings are repeated without any apparent order, emphasizing the movement of the protuberances and insets and giving the façade its distinctive look. The façade is also set off by its glazed ceramic cladding, which creates sheens and alters the shades of color. Local architecture provided the inspiration for the porticos on the ground floor–although the latter represent an element common to several architectural traditions and periods.

Architects: Oriol Bohigas, Josep Maria Martorell and David McKay

Location: Avinguda Meridiana, 312 bis-316

Date: 1959-1960

See map 2

CIC Headquarters

The headquarters of this research center required a combination of offices, laboratories and lecture rooms on a very narrow plot. A block was chosen as the quickest and most efficient solution, to avoid structural interruptions as much as possible.

Instead of opting for typical office floors with pillars, the architects decided on a structure based on a plank mold in the form of an inverted V. This design stretches right up to the top of the block, with six pillars on the side façades absorbing the thrust on the sides and also serving as finishing. This concept is visible on the main façade, making the large upside-down V the element that defines the building.

The resulting "lopsided" pillars in the interior may be out of the ordinary, but they do permit large, open spaces. On the top floor, fitted out with various laboratories, the two pillars meet to form a vertex, creating a very extensive space with a heavy structure in the center, which is highly unusual in any constructed space.

In the less visible part of the block, a small mass interrupts the form of the rectangular prism without causing any structural problems.

Architects: Guillermo Giráldez, Pedro López and Iñigo Xavier Subías

Location: Via Augusta, 205

Date: 1961

See map 3

Meridiana dog track

This dog track is situated on a quadrangular plot, with two thirds occupied by the track and the rest by Antoni Bonet's building.

This project is one of the most emblematic works of an architect classified as "purist" for his approach to both architecture and the concerns of the modern movement. This purism can be understood as a type of construction with simple lines where the structure is not only visible but is also virtually the only component in the building.

This building was put up with steel pillars to open up the ground floor as much as possible, with just a few service facilities too the rear, well away from the track. The first floor is equipped with tiered rows of seats projecting over the ground floor, as well as a large totally open space with the paraboloid lines that define its floor space left visible. The roof traces a broad arch, with a large sunscreen made of concrete sheets extending from the central section, while its ends are enclosed by large windows in aluminum frames, allowing sunlight to penetrate the offices on one side and providing a view of the terrace on the other.

Architect: Antoni Bonet

Location: Carrer Concepció Arenal, 165

Date: 1962-1963

See map 2

Torre Colón

This tower overlooking the sea houses most of the offices of the companies involved in shipping in Barcelona. In keeping with the policy in the 1960s of promoting eye-catching buildings, Josep Anglada, Daniel Gelabert and Josep Rivas came up with a daring proposal for the seafront with a skyscraper of a height similar to that of the Montjuïc mountain that dominates the port. The most obvious reference is the skyscraper complex that Le Corbusier drew up for the seafront in the 1930, but these architects' project followed another path, more in keeping with the times, with a building distinguished by its exposed concrete and expressive qualities that can be considered part of the trend toward brutalism.

The three-story rectangular mass, with an adjoining parking lot, serves as a base for the office block. This rises up to one side, with one of its vertices jutting out from the base, as if it is about to tip over. This effect is repeated throughout the building, as its faces are not flat but are slightly oblique. The pentagonal story that crowns the building endows it with a sense of movement.

Architects: Josep Anglada, Daniel Gelabert and Josep Ribas

Location: Carrer Portal de Santa Madrona, 10-12

Date: 1965-1971

See map 1

Bellvitge housing estate

The original fan-shape idea proposed by Antoni Perpiñà was not modified in the final project realized by Joan Salichs, as it provided good lighting and ventilation and efficient communication via a broad central thoroughfare. This general concept was brought to life by repeating the same type of block, with no variations or finishing touches. The blocks were built with cheap mass-produced materials and a very fast construction system that reduced costs. This resulted in buildings of a repetitive and static nature. Despite the poor quality of some parts of the complex, the neighborhood has gradually consolidated itself by incorporating services. There have recently been attempts to improve the area through the addition of new urban elements, but one of the locals' main demands—underground routes for the nearby subway and train lines—has yet to be satisfied.

These and other estates in Barcelona illustrate the rapid and chaotic growth that took place in major industrial cities in the 1960s. With the passing of the years they have given rise to neighborhoods that have found it difficult to integrate into the fabric of the city.

Architects: Juan Salichs and Antoni Perpinyà

Location: Polígono de Bellvitge (L'Hospitalet)

Date: 1966-1968

See map 1

Medical Association of Barcelona

The Medical Association of Barcelona is based in a building equipped with offices and service facilities, set in a thinly populated residential area.

The architects sought to create a distinctive building that did not need to display its institutional character via a monumental scale–in either a classical or modern idiom–and would not look out of place in a neighborhood made up of unassuming buildings. In order to fit into these surroundings, the building was conceived as the vertical sum of three different masses. These are differentiated by both offsets and projections, as well as changes in the material used to clad the façade. This broken-up appearance relates better to the small units around it than a single block would, and it also makes the building stand out sufficiently to be easily recognized.

The use of perspectives is the building's dominant feature, and so the façade fades into significance compared with the interplay of forms unleashed behind it.

Architect: Robert Terradas i Via

Location: Passeig de la Bonanova, 47

Date: 1966-1975

See map 3

Trade office blocks

This distinctive complex in a commercial district sought to break with the monotony of prismatic blocks, which is the dominant feature in the surrounding office buildings. To do this, José Antonio Coderch followed premises that reflected the concerns of the Team X (1959), which he joined in 1960. He developed two basic ideas: the relationship between the public and the private, with circulation of pedestrians, and a free use of the curtain wall. On the one hand, he decided to divide the offices into four separate blocks, bearing in mind the views and above all the flow of pedestrians between them, so that the resulting space between the four forms acts not as a square but rather as a platform on which they are set. On the other hand, Coderch explored new ideas for the curtain wall. He created a wavy homogenous surround that covers the entire building without indicating its different functions on the outer face; he was also influenced by the glass skyscrapers of Mies van der Rohe in his European phase.

This complex was one of Coderch's first office buildings, and it served for him to bring to fruition the ideas emerging from the Team X and his awareness that functionality is not an architect's sole concern but that architecture also builds its own urban setting, the landscape of the city.

Architect: José Antonio Coderch de Sentmenat

Location: Avinguda Carlos III, 92-94

Date: 1966-1969

See map 2

Torre Urquinaona

The Torre Urquinaona is one of the office buildings that were indiscriminately put up in various parts of the building in response to the law on single buildings brought in by the mayor, Josep Maria de Porcioles, which permitted much greater heights than those established by the city regulations for this type of construction.

This building designed by Antoni Bonet, like that of the Banco Atlántico—another office block put up under the same legal premises—takes the fullest possible advantage of the ground space on the corner, so, unlike most skyscrapers, its ground floor is octagonal rather than quadrangular. However, unlike the Banco Atlántico building, which is a perfect prism with a uniform façade, the Torre Urquinaona has an irregularity in three of the top floors, making it less monotonous. This change only occurs on the face overlooking Plaça Urquinaona, meaning that the insert on these three levels focuses attention on this corner and gives the impression that the building surveys the square; in this way, it becomes an integral part of the square despite its location on one of its corners.

Dark stoneware sheets were chosen for the cladding, as this material resists the pollution created by a large city.

Architects: Antoni Bonet and Josep Pui

Location: Plaça Urquinaona, 6

Date: 1966-1973

See map 1

Raset residential complex

This complex, comprising six housing blocks, was one of José Antonio Coderch's first attempts to allow the maximum penetration of sunlight into the rooms without having to reduce the depth of the homes or renounce the creation of inner patios.

The complex is organized in two rows, separated by a garden area. Each unit has a tiered outline with two distinct façades, which reflect its internal organization (a device that Coderch would use in future residential projects). Each block's rear façade gives on to an internal passageway, complete with access points, the stairwell and the elevator shaft. The main façade, overlooking the street, contains the bedrooms; the small balconies are fitted out with a lattice screen to ensure privacy, as the blocks are low and close to the street. This structure is also found on the dining-room terraces, which are larger than the other openings and close the block on the sides. The top floor is given over to an apartment with spacious terraces that has greater intimacy, on account of its height and the fact that it is set back from the rest of the façade.

Architect: José Antonio Coderch de Sentmenat

Location: Carrer Raset, 21-23

Date: 1968-1973

See map 3

Headquarters of the BBVA

This nine-story building set between party walls has successfully met the demand for extensive office space. The structure built with pillars and steel summers, makes it possible to free much of the floor space of obstacles; this has proved ideally suited to offices that have changed their internal layout over the course of the years.

The façade is finished with metal sheets and frosted-glass panels that give the building a restrained look. The modulation of the various elements with galleries on the second floor, such as the vertical strip that runs up part of the façade, reflects the interior layout while also providing a visual treatment distinct from the plain walls usually found on office blocks.

The top floor, which is set back, boasts some small garden terraces adjoining a large porch, which repeats the same structure of pillars and metal summers (here left exposed). The service facilities—including the elevator shafts, cooling system and chimneys—are grouped on the roof, hidden from view by a metal fence.

Architects: Josep Maria Fargas and Enric Tous

Location: Avinguda Diagonal, 468

Date: 1969-1973

See map 2

Coderch took advantage of the experiments he had undertaken in the Raset buildings to create a much bigger complex, in terms of both surface area and height. The big change with respect to its predecessor is the overall planning of the complex, which is much more confident and convincing.

The blocks are organized in three rows, with pedestrian walkways in between but no separation between the buildings in the same row. There are two different types of building–although these are almost identical; they alternate successively, avoiding any possible impression of monotony, while the numerous openings and offsets convey the idea of a single, unified façade.

The ground floors have now been converted into stores, but they were originally designed as homes, and so a series of flower beds was inserted to isolate them from the street, as well as to set up a rhythm that runs parallel with the façades. The complex is rounded off by a communal garage with a single entrance.

Architect: José Antonio Coderch de Sentmenat

Location: Passeig Manuel Girona, 75

Date: 1971-1973

See map 3

Fundació Joan Miró

The Foundation, situated on the Montjuïc mountain, harmoniously combines proportions based on the Modulor of Le Corbusier with the language of Mediterranean architecture. Its opening in 1975 proved an important event for Barcelona as, despite the city's international reputation, at that time it offered little in the way of cultural infrastructures. The Foundation is the trustee of the legacy of works that Joan Miró donated to the city, and it also promotes an extensive range of contemporary art.

The building was designed around two types of functions: firstly, exhibitions, with galleries and display areas, and, secondly, research, with an auditorium, a library and archives. Provisions were also made for a possible future extension, if the institution so required. While the exhibition area is characterized by the idea of an uninterrupted walk, taking in both the various galleries and the outdoor spaces—sculptures are on display in the patios, gardens and terraces—the service facilities are grouped together in a single block. The large skylights dotted all over the building provide an optimal overhead light and avoid any marked variations in illumination, while also creating a distinctive visual impact on the exterior.

Architects: Josep Lluís Sert and Jackson & Ass.

Location: Plaça de Neptú, s/n.

Date: 1972-1975

See map 1

French Institute

The French Institute building presents a very restrained approach to the office block, with an offset similar to that of the Seagram building put up in New York by Mies van der Rohe between 1954 and 1958.

Coderch created a large square in front of the building—and to a lesser extent on the sides—to isolate the Institute from the blocks around it, thereby giving it a distinctive character as a high rectangular prism designed with pure lines. This arrangement creates sufficient distance between the street and the building's façade to allow the latter to be contemplated in its totality, meaning that its simplicity can be interpreted as a sign of sobriety rather than as the overweening expression of an aggressive wall.

The ground floor acts as the base for the plane of the façade, which is marked by a rhythmic succession of rectangular windows and buttresses, of very similar proportions, allowing the building to deliberately project itself as a neutral wall. The service facilities, such as the elevator shaft, are hidden on the roof, behind a wall that follows the same proportions as the rest of the façade and is totally assimilated into it—an idea that yet again recalls van der Rohe's building in New York.

Architect: José Antonio Coderch de Sentmenat

Location: Carrer Moià, 8

Date: 1972-1974

See map 2

This school is arranged in two blocks separated by a patio in the form of an amphitheater, which serves both as an organizing element and as a functional form that comes to terms with the gradient (over 20 ft high). The classrooms in the two blocks are situated in the parts facing south-east and south-west, to take maximum advantage of the sunlight, leaving the remaining rooms for other purposes.

The idea of continuity between the patio and the spacious lobbies in both buildings is achieved by means of the expansive glass panels that act like a thin membrane wrapped around the building, without permitting their transparency to define any large volume and thereby establishing the unity of the complex. So, the amphitheater becomes a central patio that integrates the two buildings and not an area that separates them. The tiered line of the stairs marks the end of the glass front in both buildings—a deliberately brusque device on the part of the architects, who reveled in the use of materials to give the project an expressive appearance.

Architects: Oriol Bohigas, Josep Maria Martorell
and David Mckay

Location: Carretera d'Esplugues, 49-53

Date: 1972-1975

See map 3

Planeta publishing house

This building is situated in the top part of the Diagonal, an area occupied by many of the city's most important companies. This block was formerly the headquarters of the Banca Catalana.

The architects were aware of the bad reputation of office blocks and so devised an ingenious strategy for improving their image: surrounding the work areas and their façades with hanging plants. So, the building's most distinctive feature is the hanging garden that surrounds each floor, designed with exterior metal galleries that also provide room for workmen to move along them.

The publishing house occupies three octagonal buildings linked to a central, 11-floor section that houses the elevator shaft and the entrances, leaving the floors of the surrounding buildings free for workspace. The overall floor area of the complex is 285,245 sq. ft, complemented by 350 parking spaces.

The surroundings of the building are also organized in such a way that a broad expanse of greenery surrounds the building, emphasizing still further the importance of vegetation.

Architects: Josep Maria Fargas and Enric Tous

Location: Avinguda Diagonal, 662

Date: 1974-1975

See map 2

Plaça dels Països Catalans

This square was one of the first of a series of spaces that set a trend in Barcelona for so-called hard squares that rejected greenery in favor of concrete. It is situated in one of the city's most chaotic areas, like the Plaça Lesseps, and it had been untouched by any city planning before this intervention.

The architects drew up a project based on the idea of a transit area rather than a square, as the latter did not correspond to the steady flow of traffic that characterized the setting. The site projects the idea of transit through a series of elements. The paving is uniform and continuous, allowing the square to be crossed in any direction; there is no element to mark the center or endow any specificity.

This concept of transit is reinforced by the urban furnishings, such as the long, wavy porch and the wall with a window, which cuts off a series of views in the path of the pedestrians. The large pergola that characterizes the square plays a similar role in this attempt to leave the space undefined, as its height is exaggerated for the human scale and it covers a surface area that is too extensive to serve as a landmark.

Architects: Albert Viaplana and Helio Piñón

Location: Plaça dels Països Catalans, s/n

Date: 1981-1983

See map 2

Casa Serra

The Casa Serra was one of the buildings that Josep Puig i Cadafalch—a fierce critic of the rigid regularity of Cerdà's Eixample—put up on one of the irregular plots that so appealed to him. In this residential building Puig marked the axis of symmetry with a turret that serves as hinge between the two symmetrical wings. The façades on these two sides are treated differently: one of them is dominated by the main entrance, with a window and a gallery on the first floor and a continuous gallery on the second, while the other is dominated by the large balcony on the first floor, set off by another gallery on the second story and a series of arches on the ground floor.

In the 1980s the new offices of the Diputació de Barcelona (regional authority) were added to the rear; although they comprise a separate building, they are linked to the Casa Serra by a passageway, so that the old building's imposing entrance also serves as the main access to the new one.

The office block traces a neutral backdrop for the Casa Serra and echoes its volumetric design, while obviously following a different logic.

Architects: Josep Puig i Cadafalch, Federico Correa, Alfons Milà, Francesc Ribas and Javier Garrido

Location: Rambla de Catalunya, 126

Date: 1986-1988

See map 2

Plaça de la Palmera de Sant Martí

The opening-up of this square was one of several projects that were drawn up in the 1980s for areas lacking in facilities, such as this part of the Sant Martí neighborhood.

The square has two distinct sections: on one side there is a large open space designed for leisure activities and public events, while the other side is given over to a small "wood" of pine trees, planted in a regular formation that follows the curve of a sculpture by Richard Serra. This is called "Mur" (Wall), and is indeed a high concrete wall that separates the two spaces by cutting across the square. At first sight the sculpture appears to be a single continuous wall but, at the point where the enormous palm tree that gives the square its name rises up, there is a space where the wall is broken, leaving a space that joins the two sections of the square.

The large spotlight tilting over the square seems to be a clear homage to the project by El Lissitsky known as the "Lenin Tribune" (1920).

Architects: Pedro Barragán and
Bernardo de Sola

Location: Plaça de la Palmera de
Sant Martí, s/n.

Date: 1985

See map 1

Palau Sant Jordi

This project took advantage of the pronounced natural slope of the land to build some of the terracing and the multipurpose sports arena in the lower section. This variation in height is visible from the main entrance, situated in the upper part of the terracing, with the arena down below. This bold idea creates a striking image and provokes astonishment in the spectators who visit this venue.

From the outside the dome of the Palau is perceived as a form with a horizontal tendency, accentuated by the squares of the entrances on the corners and, between them, the gently undulating roof of the service facilities gallery—elements that manage to pass almost unnoticed compared with the majestic cupola that covers them.

The structure and the assembly technique were complex: the roof had to be hoisted and the rest of the building joined to it once it was mounted. Arata Isozaki was one of the first architects to take this technique to its maximum limits, although a mere ten years later it had become commonplace.

Architect: Arata Isosaki

Location: Avinguda de l'Estadi, s/n.

Date: 1985-1990

See map 1

Montjuïc Olympic Stadium

It was decided to retain the façade of the old stadium (built in 1929), to demonstrate Barcelona's Olympic aspirations, as the city had unsuccessfully applied to host the Games on two different occasions, in 1924 and 1936. This led to a modification in the design: the track was lowered to hold more spectators and meet the requirements of a modern Olympic stadium, which are much more demanding than those of the 1920s.

The stadium's façade, designed by Pere Domènech i Roura, is an example of Noucentiste architecture's use of the classical idiom, although it never became one of the most representative buildings of this movement.

The metal canopy that rears up behind the façade is a demonstration of the technical difficulties arising from the decision to keep the old façade. The superlative end results exceeded the expectations of the Games' organizers in terms of both the athletic competitions and the opening and closing ceremonies.

Architects: Vittorio Gregotti, Carles Buxadé, Federico Correa and Joan Margarit

Location: Avinguda de l'Estadi, s/n.

Date: 1986-1990

See map 1

L'Illa Diagonal

This project created a single block to house a variety of functions—such as a hotel, several offices and a shopping mall that runs through the entire building and provides much of its vitality. The elongated block repeats the same regular module in its openings to create a unified framework, although it is also broken up by variations in volume and slight offsets on the façade. These variations are determined by the scale of the elements surrounding it, while the series of windows highlights the striking unity that is maintained all along a façade of some 350 yards, so that this parallel design creates a strange contradiction that partly explains the building's great charm.

The materials and colors on the façade of the ground and first floors are different from those of the rest of the block. The shopping mall, which occupies these two floors, stretches over a long corridor with various access points on to Avinguda Diagonal, as well as exits leading on to the large garden to the rear. Other elements, such as a night club and a service area, round off the complex.

Architects: Rafael Moneo and
Manuel de Solà-Morales

Location: Avinguda Diagonal, 555-559

Date: 1986-1993

See map 2

This building evokes the idea of a Classical temple without resorting to its defining qualities, such as the understanding of an order and its use. Starting from this pseudo-classical form, where monumentalism is the essential element, the building has three distinct sections: the front access, the theater and the offices and technical departments backstage. The imposing staircase leads to an expansive glass-lined foyer, which effectively serves its purpose of handling the arrival and distribution of the audience, while also creating a comfortable setting for celebrating openings and holding receptions. Several doors open on to the 900-seat auditorium, whose dimensions give it unbeatable acoustics. The reception area is also linked to an open upper floor, with a restaurant overlooking the foyer. A rehearsal room of similar dimensions to the main stage allows two companies to work at the same time, as well as enhancing the work of the technicians and artists involved in an infrastructure of this size.

The building is set on a plot that once belonged to the state railroad company, and the tracks created a barrier between the different uses and realities of the land on either side. This duality has been maintained.

Architects: Ricardo Bofill and Taller de Arquitectura

Location: Plaça de les Arts, 13

Date: 1987-1997

See map 1

L'Auditori de Barcelona

In a single rectangular form spread over 450,000 sq. ft, L'Auditori reveals a wide range of very distinct spaces and functions. The original setting seemed to offer little potential, so Rafael Moneo came up with a compact mass closed in on itself.

This large parallelepiped is perforated by a broad walkway that opens on to an impluvium (uncovered patio), which serves as the entrance area. This configuration strives to maintain continuity between the interior and exterior spaces, as well as preserving the rigorous unity of all the façades. The impluvium suceeds in conjuring up a space of no little charm that is lit up at night and provides a view of the sky from inside the building. It also reinvents the patio as a distribution zone, merging the concepts of the town square—a meeting place within the building—and the foyer, as it has direct access to the two concert halls, with respective seating capacities of 2,340 and 610.

Other outstanding features of this project are the care taken over the acoustics required by the two concert halls and the building's capacity to fulfil very different needs: concert halls, recording studios, a center for advanced musical studies and offices.

The building's position reduces its impact, as its rigid structure within Cerdà's scheme for the Eixample interrupts the continuity between Carrer Ausiàs March and Carrer Bolívia, in a part of the city where the network of traffic connecting Besòs and Llobregat is already obstructed at other points.

Architect: Rafael Moneo

Location: Carrer Lepant, 160

Date: 1988-1998

See map 1

Mapfre Tower and Hotel Arts

The plans for the Olympic Village included the construction of two striking buildings that mark the point where Carrer Marina reaches the sea. The whole scheme represented a landmark for Barcelona, in an area that had formerly been overlooked because of its industrial character.

These two buildings were put up by two different firms, and they came up with diametrically opposed concepts for the same type of building: a rectangular prism with 40 stories. The Mapfre Tower establishes the supporting structure around the lift shaft, leaving the façade free and allowing it to be closed off with windows and wood and aluminum finishings, which vaguely recall the world of the sailboats docked in the nearby port.

In contrast, the structure of the Hotel Arts is a large three-dimensional exterior mesh, which gives the building a more solid look. The view from the beach is an accurate proposition for an area where tower blocks meet the sea, as it is rounded off by a stark square devoid of scenery on an upper level and a series of small stores below, all just a few yards from the sandy beach.

Architects: Mapfre Tower: Íñigo Ortiz a Enrique León. Hotel Arts: SOM Studio

Location: Carrer Marina, 16-19

Date: 1988-1993

See map 1

The glass façade of the Contemporary Art Museum of Barcelona (MACBA) opens up the interior to the street while also providing views of the adjacent, newly created square from the inside.

Some elements break the monotony of the parallelopiped: on the one hand, a wavy mass with no openings at one end, with an exhibition space inside; on the other, at the opposite end of the block, the entrance appears as a vertical plane superimposed on the rest of the façade, offering glimpses of the terrace hidden behind through its various openings. This section, which also contains the offices, does not follow the layout of the main block but is joined to it by an elevated passageway. The vertical organisation is set apart from the interior space, with three different axes for reaching the different levels: a spiral staircase, an elevator in another part of the building (in the service area) and a long ramp with a gentle slope in front of the large glass façade, offering a leisurely climb that gives visitors a chance to enjoy the view of the square before entering the museum's main hall.

Architect: Richard Meier

Location: Plaça dels Àngels, s/n

Date: 1988-1995

See map 1

Collserola Tower

.

This tower, 945-ft high, is situated on a spot called Turó de Vilana in the Collserola mountains, 1,460 ft above sea level.

It is a communications tower comprising a large spike emerging from a central triangular section 130 ft from the ground; this is secured by two cables that are attached to the spike and the base of the tubular column underneath. Other steel braces extend from the three vertices of the triangle and are fixed to the ground, thereby providing stability.

The central structure comprises 13 platforms. The tenth one serves as a viewing platform that enables members of the public to enjoy the stunning panoramic views of the city. This level is reached by an elevator running down the outside of the shaft joining the platforms to the ground. The project is completed with a series of underground service facilities in the base.

The tower's structure was built at the same time as the Palau Sant Jordi, and both became symbols of modernisation. Furthermore, the positioning of the tower reflects the concept of the city as a territory by dominating both sides of the mountain range, thereby embracing the whole region currently included in Barcelona's metropolitan area.

Architect: Norman Foster

Location: Carretera de Vallvidrera al Tibidabo, s/n.

Date: 1989-1992

See map 3

The plans to redevelop part of the Poble Nou neighborhood as a bold contribution to the 1992 Olympic Games project revolved around a series of buildings-gateways that mark the access points to the Olympic Village.

This building, conceived as a free interpretation of the city gate, is influenced by both the Paris Customs House, designed by Chris Ledoux and Etienne-Louis Boulée, and Robert Venturi's book "Learning from Las Vegas" (1962), whose ideas marked an entire generation of architects and gave a new dimension to the significance of architecture.

This building provided an imaginative and extremely practical way to insert offices in an area that was otherwise exclusively given over to the construction of accommodation for the athletes taking part in the Olympics. This office block forms an inverted staircase, with barely noticeable supports on one side and a horizontal top that sets off the striking design of its tiered silhouette.

Architects: Albert Viaplana and Helio Piñón

Location: Carrer Rosa Sensat/Avinguda Icària

Date: 1989-1992

See map 1

Olympic Village

The area now covered by the Olympic Village was once an industrial zone crossed by a railroad track that formed an insuperable barrier to the rest of the city, while another track ran alongside the sea, effectively making Barcelona a city with no beaches that turned its back on the sea. It was decided to reclaim this land to build accommodation for the athletes competing in the Olympic Games. This redevelopment eliminated both the railroad tracks and constructed a boulevard along the sea front. The layout of Cerdà's Eixample was respected, albeit with several variations, such as the placement of family houses inside the blocks and of thin buildings around the perimeters.

The general plan, drawn up by the studio of Oriol Bohigas, Josep Maria Martorell, David McKay and Albert Puigdomènech, took many other factors into account, such as the communications axes—with the Ronda Litoral being put underground—and the use of two different scales, one for the low-density residential section and one for the Olympic port, with its two towers standing as symbols of the new city.

Architects: Antoni Bonet and Taller Bofill

Location: Carrer Amsterdam, s/n.

Date: 1989-1992

See map 1

Vall d'Hebron residential complex

This residential complex was built to house the journalists that covered the Olympic Games in Barcelona; the apartments were subsequently sold as private homes.

The complex is one of the most recent constructions on the western side of the Vall d'Hebron and it adapted to the lay of the land by using two different types of building (although these are closely related). The lower and flatter part of the plot is given over to homes distributed around the Plaça Joan Cornudella, with two tower blocks flanking the street. Another block unwinds perpendicular to the slope, with a thoroughfare on one side and a pedestrian garden area on the other, directly linked to the square.

The sinuous form of this block is set off by high piles that signal the access to the garden area and block the entrance to cars. The façade, marked by horizontal strips, overlooks the curving road; it is not adapted to the unevenness of the terrain, and the architects managed to achieve an overall sense of unity without drawing attention to the changes in height between the different sections.

Architects: Carlos Ferrater, Josep Maria Carañá, Joan Forcadell, Ferran Pla and Robert Suso

Location: Carrer Berruguete/Plaça Joan Cornudella

Date: 1989-1991

See map 3

Botanical Garden

The Botanical Garden is an ambitious project to create a center that displays and investigates various forms of plant life and their environments. It is set in one of the most forgotten areas of the Montjuïc mountain, designed as a grid of triangular sections that adapt to the terrain and recreate several ecosystems to highlight a wide range of plant species. The idea of triangular sections is echoed in the various buildings that stake out the garden, such as the entrance portico, built as if it was just another part of the grid spread over the land. The various routes that are signposted in the park are marked out by the vertices of these triangles, with the exception of the first section, where a walkway runs over a marshy area, thereby breaking up the triangular grid, which is only suggested by the iron buttresses that run alongside.

The garden is constantly evolving as a result of the meticulous modification and observation of the different environments, in order to adapt them to the various species, and it will continue to change as the present plants grow, or as new ones are introduced.

Architects: Carlos Ferrater, Josep Lluís Canosa and Elisabeth Figueras

Location: Montjuïc mountain

Date: 1989-2001

See map 1

Archery range

The two buildings meet to form a "V" shape. They were intended for use by archers in the Olympic Games, and their unusual design left a large open space for the fan-shape archery range, as well as making it easy to pass from one building to another. However, only one of the buildings was intended for Olympic competition, as the other was exclusively reserved for training. Even though their forms are very different, the idea behind the whole complex was weightlessness and defiance of the horizontal line. One of the buildings was built with prefabricated concrete slabs that cover both the walls and the roof, while the other is based on a series of wavy roofs supported by double pillars in the form of an inverted V–with the vertex supporting the roof–which leave the wall free of any loads, meaning that it serves merely to define the interior and exterior spaces.

These buildings, which have been poorly maintained, have now been converted into dressing rooms and services for a sports center, and the archery range itself turned into two soccer pitches.

Architects: Enric Miralles and Carme Pinós

Location: Carrer Basses d'Horta/Avinguda Martí de Codolar

Date: 1990-1991

See map 3

The radical refurbishment of an old convent and orphanage resulted in a totally pragmatic and convenient building, it's which houses Center of Contemporary Culture of Barcelona (CCCB).

The conversion respects the original building's layout around a large central patio, although it did modify one side to renovate the structure. The new wing forms the institution's vertical axis, with elevators and escalators connecting the main foyer—which lies underground, below the patio, and is reached by a gentle slope—and the rest of the building. Its façade rises up with a new three-story addition, complete with a vertiginous overhang and a glass front that serves as a mirror for onlookers at the base of the building, reflecting a stunning view of the city—the same as the one that can be enjoyed by visitors inside the building. The paving of the patio and the glass on the façade comes in two different colors. The glass panels on the eastern side are transparent, while on the western side, which is more exposed to sunlight, they are slightly tinted, in order to filter the heat in the summer.

Architects: Albert Viaplana and Helio Piñón

Location: Carrer Montalegre, 5

Date: 1990-1994

See map 1

Maremagnum

The conversion of dilapidated trading depots into a shopping mall-leisure center was largely promoted by the City Hall. The aim was to create a complex that was remote from residential districts, to avoid any possible disturbance, and also to take advantage of the significant commercial benefits of an operation on this scale.

It is interesting to observe how the format of a shopping mall—the format that best defines our era—is capable of adapting to any setting in Western society, even an old industrial port.

The complex is extremely popular, thanks to the walkway over the sea drawn up by Albert Viaplana and Helio Piñón, which acts as a prolongation of the Rambla—hence the project's title Rambla de Mar (Rambla of the Sea). The walkway is designed as a quay with wavy forms, with some parts acting as wooden "beaches" with a series of benches on the seafront, protected from the area's constant winds by transparent glass panels.

The construction of this walkway and the redevelopment of the Moll de la Fusta and Barceloneta finally opened the city up to the sea in the 1990s.

Architects: Albert Viaplana and Helio Piñón

Location: Moll de les Drassanes

Date: 1990-19995

See map 1

Fecsa Headquarters

The office block for this electrical company was put up on the site of an old plant. The three chimneys of the original building have been preserved, both for their identification with their company and as a very dynamic visual element in the old city.

The complex is divided into three large blocks that maintain an industrial look, particularly the biggest block, with its exposed structure of cement and exposed metalwork overshadowing the tinted glass windows, as well as providing easy access to clean them and making the façade simpler to maintain. Perpendicular to this block, a lower building stands in front of the chimneys, in keeping with the first, as it is made with similar modules and an exposed concrete structure. A third block is situated at a short distance from these two, with a curtain wall finished with dark windows and enclosures, and flanked by a fountain and a large pond that sets off an interplay with the reflections of the wall on the water.

The expressiveness of this complex stands out in this area near the mountain, characterised by low buildings, and it creates a backdrop that does not overshadow its surroundings.

Architects: Pere Riera, Josep Maria Gutiérrez, Josep Sotorres and Montserrat Batlle

Location: Avinguda Paral·lel, 51-53

Date: 1990-1993

See map 1

Montjuïc Telecommunications Tower

The telecommunications tower was the only element that was not planned in the original project for this area, and it was skilfully integrated into its setting, with a sculptural outline painted in spotless white that adapts to the lay of the land in front of the Palau Sant Jordi. The tower is conceived as an urban element, despite its height of 394 ft. At first sight it does not look like a communications tower, as the hemispherical panels typical of satellite antennae are hidden from view and its striking, playful form is extremely unconventional.

The most surprising element is the mast, which recalls the tilt of the Earth's axis—meaning that it can also serve as a solar clock—and creates a balance with the antenna, which is surrounded by a ring that houses the majority of the technical equipment. The base, reinforced by the tilt of the mast, operates as a counterweight, as it is embedded in the ground, giving a sense of weightlessness to the two structure, which is essentially two pieces with an opening between them.

The technical mastery of the engineer-architect Santiago Calatrava is evident in this elegant construction; it is visible from the Montjuïc mountain and from other parts of the city, but it never overshadows the original buildings surrounding it.

Architect: Santiago Calatrava

Location: Avinguda de l'Estadi, s/n.

Date: 1991

See map 1

Nexus Building

This office building, set in the university campus, was destined to be an organising element despite its relatively small size. Instead of trying to affirm the presence of the offices, the architect chose to hide them behind a glass screen with no visible fittings that reflects its surroundings. This approach succeeded in creating a striking element in the landscape that will nevertheless blend in well with any new additions to the landscape.

The access points in this imposing cylinder are two simple quadrangular concrete openings, with a ramp made of the same material. A small lawn embankment encircles the building, providing a visual transition between the surrounding buildings and the reflecting walls.

Inside, two patios allow sunlight to flood into most of the offices. The various gardens in the interior seek to provide a personal touch to each department and offset the coldness of the façade.

Architect: Lluís Nadal

Location: Carrer Gran Capità, 2-4

Date: 1992-1995

See map 3

Housing on Carrer Carme

This building is situated in a very densely populated part of the old city. The architect, Josep Llinàs, developed an unusual strategy by breaking down the block into various sections to ensure that the apartments received sunlight, but without reducing the overall number of homes. The ground floor occupies almost the entire terrain, except for the corner, where it folds inwards in order to provide more room on this long, narrow street, and also to add a distinctive visual flourish. Vertically, the building is divided into three blocks, and the separation between them allows for optimum ventilation and a greater exposure to light than that provided by a typical inner patio. It thereby offers a new approach to construction in old city centers, and its very existence could be seen to represent as a criticism of the excessive demolition taking place in this neighborhood under the banners of greater salubriousness and improved flow of traffic.

The importance of empty space in this project reflects the concepts of city planning, albeit on a smaller scale. The high quality of the result is accompanied by a formal language common to most of today's architects.

Architect: Josep Llinàs

Location: Carrer Carme, 5

Date: 1992-1995

See map 1

Palau de Congressos

This building is made of three differentiated sections separated by two inner roads that run between them and link the rear gardens with the façade on Avinguda Diagonal.

The first section, to the right of the main block, contains a large foyer, an auditorium with a seating capacity of 2,500 and, beneath this, a banquet hall. The second, smaller module, boasts a large multi-purpose space with mobile walls on the ground floor and an upper level with enormous adjustable skylights. A thin strip on the end of the plot houses a nightclub, various offices and access to the underground parking lot.

The treatment of the façade and the interior finishings bestow a sober elegance on a building of this type, which is usually characterised by its monotony. It also manages to set up a relationship with its surroundings, in an area where Diagonal is more of a freeway than a street, and it succeeds in creating a human scale inside, despite its large open spaces and the fact that the exterior is governed by the traffic.

Architect: Carles Ferrater

Location: Avinguda Diagonal, 661

Date: 1996-2000

See map 2

Universitat Pompeu Fabra

The university campus is organized around the Parc de la Ciutadella. There are plans to move the zoo that occupies most of the park outside the city, leaving the space as an element that integrates the buildings around it.

The university was set in Jaume I's former military barracks, dating from the second half of the 19th century (and refurbished for their present purpose), and the park's old water plant, the work of Josep Fontserè and the young Antoni Gaudí.

Even though the barracks were converted, they maintained their configuration around the patios, which serve to distribute the flow of passersby. One of the most significant changes was the transformation of Carrer Doctor Trueta between the two blocks of the old barracks. This street was formerly protected by high walls but it is now an open pedestrian thoroughfare providing access to the university. The basement is fitted out with a space for reflection and meditation designed by Antoni Tàpies and Jordi Garcès.

Architects: Esteve Bonell and Josep Maria Gil

Location: Carrer Ramon Trias Fargas, 27

Date: 1996-1997

See map 1

Gràcia Library

This project involved the construction of a large library on a small plot, and so it had to be developed on a vertical plane. In order to avoid creating a series of identical stories, Josep Llinàs accentuated the communication between the levels and open spaces, thereby creating visual continuity, albeit minimal. This idea is repeated on the façade, with large glass windows leaving extensive parts of the interior open to view, emphasizing the public function of the building. The treatment of the façade, with its striking sgraffito in different alphabets, enhances this permeability: the unbroken wall goes unnoticed as all the attention is focused on the openings. The reception on the ground floor becomes a prolongation of the street, visible through the main entrance or the large glass walls.

It is interesting to compare this building with the same architect's Fort Pienc Civic Center, as despite the huge differences in the settings and functions, and in the strategies used to make them work as public spaces, they show similar concerns and the results are equally successful.

Architect: Josep Llinàs

Location: Travessera de Gràcia/Carrer Torrent de l'Olla

Fecha: 2002

See map 2

Fort Pienc Civic Center

Josep Llinàs used an architectural language that owes much to new techniques and calculations of structures to create a single block that contains several public services for the Fort Pienc neighborhood: a civic center, a library, a crèche, a senior citizens' residence, public housing apartments, a market and a supermarket.

The project is characterized by its attention to urban planning, with a skilful offset of the façade on Carrer Ribes to create a square that has become a popular meeting place for the locals. This space leads to the civic center and library and, at another point, to the underground supermarket and market, designed as a corridor that crosses the building before opening out on to Carrer Alí Bei. The senior citizens' residence is set on one corner of the complex, with a large flat roof on top of the market and an interior entrance that provides direct access to the civic center and the library. The library section, in the form of an L, closes the square off on one side; it is characterized by a spacious terrace on the second floor, covered by a projecting third story.

Architect: Josep Llinàs

Location: Carrer Ribes, 14

Date: 2003

See map 1

Parc Litoral Nord-Est

This space on the outer edge of the city, by the mouth of the River Besós, has been drawn up to house a treatment plant for organic refuse, a youth hostel, a series of commercial premises near the beach and an artificial hillside that disguises a number of service facilities. None of these constructions detract from the underlying concept of a park with a wood, sand dunes and a beach that also blends in with the industrial buildings in the area.

The hillside, on the face away from the sea, offers some stunning views of the complex, as well as isolating it from the noise pollution created by the Ronda Litoral. From here there is a choice of two different routes: one to a large open space by the port and youth hostel on the banks of the river—which acts as a screen for the industrial area—and another to a large coppice that dominates its surroundings.

Various facilities have been pragmatically integrated into a picturesque vision of the setting, complete with walks, remains of industrial ruins and dramatic scenery.

Architects: Iñaki Ábalos and Juan Herreros.
Mosaic: Albert Oehlen

Location: Parc Litoral

Date: 2000-2004

See map 1

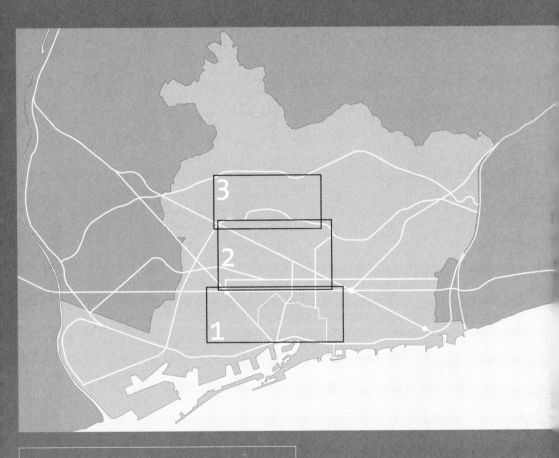

Barcelona

‹ 202

66

Gran Via de les Corts Catalanes

Plaça
d'Espanya

168

25

242

Avinguda de la reina Maria Cristina

Sant Antoni

142

Ronda Sant Pau

16 Carrer del Carme

154

148

Carrer de l'Hospital

Ronda

152

Avinguda

262

230

232

216

14 Carrer de Sant Pau

Parallel

Montjuic

mountain

Carrer Nou de la Rambla

260

200

252

28

Plaça de la
Carbonera

The number indicated on the map corresponds to the page on which the project appears in the guide

map 1

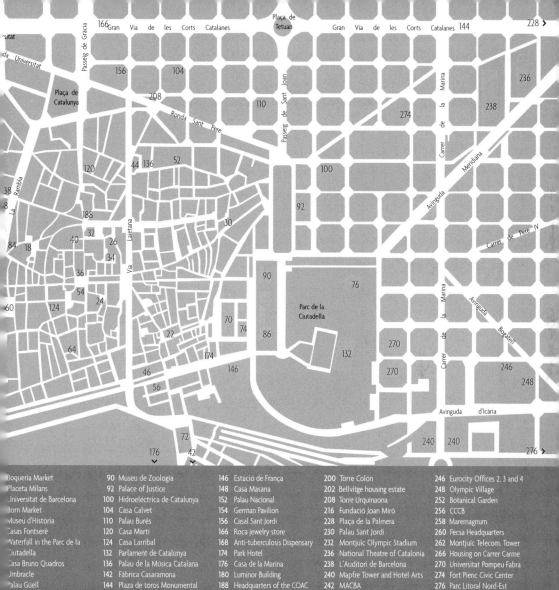

The number indicated on the map corresponds to the page on which the project appears in the guide

map 2

<290

Passeig de la Bonanova
204

Carrer de la Salle

Passeig de Sant Gervasi

Plaça de John F. Kennedy

^244 ^114

Carrer de Balmes

Via Augusta

<264

<94

<220 214 192

<186

96 Ronda del General Mitre

210

Via Augusta

196

Plaça de Prat de la Riba

Av. Carles III

Carrer de Balmes

The number indicated on the map corresponds to the page on which the project appears in the guide

map 3

Architecture, guides and city planning

- Cerdà, Ildefons: "The General Theory of Urbanization". Imprenta Española, Madrid, 1856.

- Hernàndez-Cros, Juli Emili; Mora, Gabriel and Pouplana, Xavier: "Arquitectura de Barcelona". Col·legi d'Arquitectes de Catalunya, Barcelona, 1990.

- Laboratori d'Urbanisme: "Treballs sobre Cerdà i el seu Eixample a Barcelona". Ajuntament de Barcelona, Barcelona, 1992.

- Tolosa, Lluís and Montes, Cristina: "Barcelona Style". H. Kliczkowski, Barcelona, 2001.

- Gausa, Manuel; Cervelló, Marta and Pla, Maurici: "Architecture Guide to Barcelona: 1860-2001". ACTAR, Barcelona, 2002.

- Von Heeren, Stefanie: "Un análisis crítico del modelo de Barcelona: la remodelación de Ciutat Vella". Universidad del País Vasco, Vitoria, 2002.

- Various authors: "HICAT: HiperCatalunya: Research Territories". ACTAR, Barcelona, 2003.

- Cuito, Aurora: "Enric Miralles/Benedetta Taglibue". H. Kliczkowski, Barcelona, 2003.

- Bonet, Llorenç: "Josep Lluís Sert/Joan Miró". H. Kliczkowski, Barcelona, 2003.

Children's literature

- Rifà, Fina and Cormand, Bernat: "Barcelona tell us about Gaudí". H. Kliczkowski, Barcelona, 2002.

Literature and essays

- Mendoza, Eduardo: "The City of Marvels". Seix Barral, Barcelona, 1988.

- Various authors: "Barcelona, un dia". Extra Alfaguara, Madrid, 1998.

- Guillamon, Julià: "La ciutat interrompuda. De la contracultura a la Barcelona postolímpica". La Magrana, Barcelona, 2001.

- Various authors: "Nazario: Barcelona 1972-2002". Ajuntament de Barcelona. Barcelona, 2002.

- Millet, Joaquim: "No me rayes". Galería H2O, Barcelona, 2002.

Movies

- Pons, Ventura: "Ocaña, retrat intermitent". 1978.

- Aranda, Vicente: "Si te dicen que caí". 1989.

- Almodóvar, Pedro: "All about my mother". 1999.

- Guerín, José Luís: "En construcción". 2000.

Web

- www.bcn.es/urbanisme/

Other titles by the publisher

La Fundición, 15 Polígono Industrial Santa Ana 28529 Rivas-Vaciamadrid Madrid Spain
Tel. 34 91 666 50 01 Fax 34 91 301 26 83 asppan@asppan.com www.onlybook.com

Gaudí, arquitectura modernista
en Barcelona/Gaudí, Modernist
Architecture in Barcelona
ISBN: (E) 84-96048-16-0
ISBN: (GB) 84-96048-17-9

Barcelona de noche
Barcelona by Night
ISBN: (E) 84-89439-71-0
ISBN: (GB) 84-89439-72-9

Gaudí. Obra completa
Gaudí. Complete works
ISBN (E): 84-89439-90-7
ISBN (GB): 84-89439-91-5
ISBN (CAT): 84-96137-29-5
ISBN (F): 84-96048-41-1

Barcelona, Gaudí y la Ruta
del Modernismo
ISBN: (E) 84-89439-50-8
ISBN: (GB) 84-89439-51-6
ISBN: (D) 84-89439-58-3
ISBN: (IT) 84-89439-59-1
ISBN: (JP) 84-89439-60-5

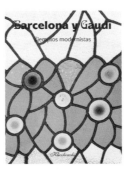

Barcelona y Gaudí. Ejemplos
modernistas/Barcelona and Gaudí.
Examples of modernist architecture
ISBN: (E) 84-89439-64-8
ISBN: (GB) 84-89439-65-6

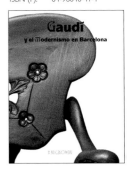

Gaudí y el Modernismo en
Barcelona/Gaudí and
Modernism in Barcelona
ISBN: (E) 84-89439-50-8
ISBN: (GB) 84-89439-51-6